Street Food

Urban foraging and world food

Ceridwen Buckmaster

GW00492874

Designed by Dorothea Bohlius
Photos by Nemo Roberts

Invisible Press London

First published by Invisible Press, 2013

ISBN 978-0-9927729-0-1

Published by
Invisible Press
Flat 16 Myatts Field Court
18 Mcdowall Road
London
SE5 9JS

For more copies of this book: invisiblefood@gmail.com

Designed by Dorothea Bohlius
Photos by Nemo Roberts
Artwork preparation by Ibuki Iwata
Editorial support by Martha Brown, Sam Jarvis and Nick Neale
Pinted and bound by Media CPM, Colchester

Additional photos
Ceridwen Buckmaster 5, 8, 20, 24, 26, 30, 34, 49, 54, 64, 77, 92, 96, 97, 100, 110
Dorothea Bohlius 19, 21, 22, 31, 58, 61, 70, 72
Meredith Rosenbluth 12, 13, 14,
Jorge Goia 16, 74
Carolyn Gaskell 44, 51
Madeleine Geach 102
Melanie Clifford 50
Freya Macosborne 84

Please note:
The plant information in Street Food: Urban foraging and World food has been
written from a mixture of folk information and modern herbal medicine practice
as well as from personal experience. It is not intended to replace the advice
and care of a qualified herbal or medical practitioner. Pay particular attention if you
are already taking prescribed medicines or are pregnant, and seek professional
advice before using herbs as medicine. Plants are powerful!

The people who created this book

Nemo Roberts, Dorothea Bohlius, Ceridwen Buckmaster, Ibuki Iwata

Ceridwen Buckmaster, Author

Ceri is a writer and community facilitator who explores how it is possible to respond creatively to economic, spiritual and environmental crises. Her projects bring to the fore conversations, relationships and informal networks that are often undervalued or invisible in society. She met Dorothea and Ibuki while all their children were at the South London cooperative nursery Childpsace.
www.ceribuckmaster.co.uk

Dorothea Bohlius, Designer

Dorothea is a graphic designer who loves to develop design concepts and to indulge in good food. In her work, she enjoys capturing the concept of a project, or in the case of this book, the essence of a dish, in unique and elegant ways.
www.dorotheabohlius.carbonmade.com

Nemo Roberts, Photographer

Nemo is a photographer who loves the environmental, creative, nutritional and emotional aspects of food. She also writes about British food and culture for Japanese media. She left Tokyo in 2003, and is currently based in London. She is about to begin J42, a cookery book of Japanese food for two.
www.nemoroberts.wordpress.com/about-nemo

Ibuki Iwata, Artwork preparation

Ibuki is a freelance graphic designer, specialising in branding design. She loves the challenge of expressing invisible ideas in visuals. She is also a keen Origami practitioner and a teacher.
ibukiiwata@gmail.com

Introduction

Street Food: Urban foraging and world food shines a spotlight on wild food as 'the new street food' in a collection of recipes inspired by the wild plants that grow in urban areas, as well as by the people and the diverse food traditions present in the city.

What I am referring to as Street Food is the wild food found in urban space; safe places like parks (away from dog walked areas), and not on old industrial sites. Street Food also refers to the urban culture of eating food on the go. It fills you up and keeps you going on a busy day. The culture of Street Food contributes to the atmosphere, safety and conviviality of our urban centres.

The idea for this book developed out of the project Invisible Food. For me, Invisible Food refers to everything that sustains us that isn't ordinarily visible. The 'food' is the wild foods such as nettle or elderflower that we can harvest and learn how to use. However, there is also a deeper, more soulful interpretation of invisible food as something that sustains us emotionally and spiritually, and creates a strong community and a connection with the earth.

Friendliness, generosity, time spent walking, talking and sharing food together all create safety.

Throughout the project, groups of people have experimented with each other's cooking traditions and with common wild plants such as nettle, chickweed, and dandelion. We have made dumplings, stews, pickles and breads; dishes which are common around the world. Throughout history, as people have moved and been moved around the globe, the food they eat has been adapted and many dishes have taken root in cultures far away from where they originated. We explore wild food versions of some dishes that are symbols of historical forces. For example, the Vietnamese *bánh mì* sandwich, which is a result of the French introducing bread and *paté* to Vietnam, and the Venezuelan Christmas dish, *Hallaca,* which is a coming together of European, Native American and African traditions. The recipes in the book are mainly vegetarian, but sometimes contain fish, if this is essential in the traditional recipe.

There are many ingredients in the recipes that aren't wild and need to be bought in a shop. This book isn't a venture in trying to live off wild food alone. While the main premise is how to cook wild plants in exciting ways, it's also about how to prepare food that connects you to a community of people with diverse backgrounds, who are living in the same place as you and sharing the same resources.

Many fruit trees have been planted over recent years in London.

What we eat is one way to directly connect to the life forces of the planet, and the more we engage with the processes of food harvesting and preparation, the more we can be mindful about our connection to the earth. While there are some glorious built-in safeguards in nature to ensure equal distribution of food; for example holly berries are toxic to humans but not to birds, we humans have to learn how to take consciously, to learn how much is enough and to leave what other creatures need more than us. It's certainly not my intention to create a fad of wild food that destroys our wildlife. Please always check with yourself if you will use what you pick and never pick more than a third of the plant. Similarly, to avoid wastage, I try to look after seeds once I've collected them. I keep them in a suitable bag, shake them regularly and look out for signs that they might need some other form of storage.

The connection with knowing our true needs averts the danger of being mechanical, negligent and prone to wastage in our interactions with nature. It is when human beings stop checking what they really need, that abuse and exploitation of the environment occurs, leading ultimately to scarring the earth's surface through mining and cutting down the rainforest.

To mark the process of recognising and acknowledging our true needs, there is an 'Ingredient for Soul Food' at the end of each chapter. This is a quiet reflection on the experience of creating community walks and feasts, as well as the 'ingredients' necessary to do this. These ingredients are inspired by the human needs articulated in Marshall Rosenberg's Nonviolent communication. My hope is that this book is part of a process that strengthens and connects us in our communities, and that you do what your parents always told you not to do ... start playing with your food!

Contents

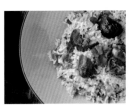

South East Asia

Recipes from Thailand, Vietnam and Malaysia

**Spicy Malaysian goosegrass
with dried shrimp**

Pickled goosegrass stems

Chickweed salad with spicy dressing

**Vietnamese *bánh mì* with chickweed
and wild herb *paté***

Rice wraps with wild winter herbs

Chickweed
Stellaria media

**Goosegrass
or Cleavers**
Galium aparine

Wild food in January

Chickweed
What it looks like: 5 star-like petals, cordate (heart-shaped) leaves grow in pairs on opposite sides of the stem. Vivid, mid-green colour. Single line of hairs run up one side of stem, changing side at each pair of leaves.
How it can be useful: It is high in calcium, vitamins A, C and potassium and can be eaten raw in salads, or wilted like spinach. Chickweed has been used for fevers, inflammations, chest congestion, lung infections, bronchitis and eczema.

Goosegrass or Cleavers
What it looks like: Sprawling stems have 4 angles and feel like a square. There are 6–8 narrow elliptical or lanceolate leaves in a whorl around the stem. Hooked hairs on its leaves and fruit 'cleave' to clothes.
How it can be useful: Stir fry or make into soups. Goosegrass is a diuretic and increases the flow of urine. It has been used for cystitis, kidney inflammation and irritable bladders. It helps rid the lymphatic system of waste.

Spicy Malaysian goosegrass with dried shrimp

500g (1lb) fresh goosegrass stems

4 garlic cloves

25g (1oz) fresh root ginger, peeled and chopped

2 red chillies, seeded and chopped

2 tablespoons dried shrimp, soaked in warm water to rehydrate, drained

1 teaspoon shrimp paste

2 tablespoons vegetable or groundnut oil

1 teaspoon palm sugar

2 tablespoons light soy sauce

Goosegrass and chickweed are both good substitutes for Kangkung, which is the Malay name for water spinach or morning glory, and is used across South East Asia. Like water spinach, goosegrass and chickweed love wet winter conditions.   **Serves 4**

1 Using a pestle and mortar, grind the garlic, ginger and chillies to a smooth paste. Add the dried shrimp and shrimp paste and bind with a little oil.

2 Heat the rest of the oil in a heavy pan. Stir in the paste and cook for 2-3 minutes over a low heat. Stir in the sugar and soy sauce.

3 Add the goosegrass stems and stir briefly before adding a lid to the pan and allowing the leaves to wilt for 2 minutes only.

4 Serve immediately with rice.

Pickled goosegrass stems

1 large handful
goosegrass stems

2 teaspoons salt

4 garlic cloves

2oz (50g) sugar

200ml (7fl oz) suka
(Filipino coconut
vinegar) or
pickling vinegar

1 Make the pickling solution by combining the salt, crushed garlic cloves, vinegar and sugar in a pan and heating to dissolve sugar gently. Allow to cool.

2 Prepare the stems. Cut each stem into small pieces about 5cm (2in) long. Wash, drain and dry completely.

3 Put the stems into a jar. Add the pickling solution and leave for a day or two before serving.

3 Use in the Vietnamese *bánh mì* dish.

Vietnamese *bánh mì* with chickweed and wild herb *paté*

A large handful of chickweed

4 small finger rolls

1 small tub wild herb paté

1 packet marinated and fried tofu

Thin jalapeño pepper slices (optional)

Pickled goosegrass stems (see previous recipe)

Wild herb paté

Large handful of chickweed and goosegrass

1 large onion

2 large tomatoes

1 teaspoon thyme

4 cloves garlic

75g (3oz) cashew nuts

1 small chilli, chopped

Tofu

300g (10oz) firm tofu

90ml (3fl oz) veg oil

2 cloves garlic

5 tablespoons soy sauce

1 teaspoon sesame oil

1 handful sorrel leaves

This is an interesting fusion of French bread and paté, and Vietnamese herbs and seasoning. I've replaced lemongrass with the lemony tang of sorrel. Serves 4

Wild herb *paté*
1 Sweat the onion in oil until translucent. Chop the tomatoes and add to the onions, along with the chilli and thyme. Cook for 5 minutes. Chop the chickweed and goosegrass finely and add.
2 Simmer with a lid on for another 5 minutes, adding some water so the mixture doesn't stick.
3 Meanwhile, grind the nuts very finely. Add them at the end of the cooking time and stir well. Liquidise everything together to make a smooth paté.

Tofu
1 Slice tofu into pieces about 1cm thick.
2 Combine chopped sorrel leaves, crushed garlic, vegetable oil, soy sauce, sesame oil and season with salt and pepper. Mix the marinade well and add slices of tofu. Make sure each slice of tofu is coated. Marinade for at least 1 hour.
3 Fry the tofu. You won't need any more oil as the marinade is very oily. Fry until both sides are golden brown with a nice firm crust. Let cool.

Assemble the *bánh mì* sandwich
1 Spread paté on the insides of the roll. On one slice of the roll, add the tofu, and spread with mayonnaise if using. Add the chickweed, the goosegrass pickle and jalapeño pepper on top.
2 Close the roll to sandwich the fillings together and serve.

Chickweed salad with spicy dressing

A large handful
chickweed

1 small onion, thinly
sliced

½ teaspoon toasted
sesame seeds

Spicy dressing

2 tablespoons
vegetable oil

2 garlic cloves,
finely chopped

4 tablespoons
lemon juice

2 tablespoons
caster sugar

1 tablespoon fish sauce
or tamari

1 chilli, finely chopped

Water dropwort is often used as a salad ingredient in many Asian countries. However, water dropwort in Europe is poisonous. Later on in the season, we could replace with cow parsley but this is not easy to distinguish for a beginner forager, so we'll use chickweed instead for a refreshing salad. Salads in Asia often incorporate wilted leaves but here I do them raw.   Serves 4

1 Mix all the ingredients for the dressing and whisk briefly.
2 Put leaves in a bowl, add the onion and the dressing.
3 Garnish with toasted sesame seeds and serve.

Rice wraps with wild winter herbs

1 packet of rice wraps

A handful of chickweed and dandelion leaves

A handful of sorrel leaves

1 red pepper, chopped into long strips

1 spring onion, chopped into long strips

Nuoc Cham sauce

75g (3oz) caster sugar

125ml (4fl oz) fish sauce or tamari

250ml (8fl oz) hot water

1 tablespoon white rice vinegar

60ml (2fl oz) lime juice

2 red chillies, chopped

3 cloves garlic, chopped

The sweet red pepper combines well with the bitter dandelion and the refreshing chickweed. You can prepare all the wraps in advance or have the rice-wrapping as something your community does together, with everyone making their own wraps. For this you just need space.

1 Place all the filling ingredients in separate bowls. Prepare a dish of water that is bigger than the diameter of the rice wraps and immerse a wrap in the dish of water for about 20 seconds. If you leave it too long, it'll get too sticky to work with. If you don't leave it long enough, it won't stick to itself to seal the wrap. Remove it from the water and place on a plate.

2 Place some strips of red pepper and spring onion horizontally on the bottom half of the wrap nearest you. Add some chick-weed stems, and dandelion and sorrel leaves.

3 Fold up the bottom of the wrap over the filling. Fold in the left and right sides. Roll the wrap over itself until it has closed. You can also leave one end open to see the leaves inside. Dip in sauce and eat.

Nuoc Cham sauce

1 Put the sugar in a bowl and pour the hot water over it, stirring until dissolved. Add the other ingredients, stir and let cool. This will keep in the fridge for a week.

Structure and safety

"*If you're encouraging people to do something they don't normally do (eg. connect with new people, walk in a part of town they would never normally go to, eat something different) they need to feel safe physically and emotionally, otherwise they'll just go home.*

What a community project needs above all else is to be clear. Some kind of clear structure and predictability will help people feel safe and able to participate.

Friendliness, generosity, time spent walking, talking and sharing food together all create safety."

FEBRUARY

East Africa

Recipes from Ethiopia, Eritrea and Somalia

**Wild rocket, wild cabbage
and garlic mustard sprouted seeds**

East African wild greens

***Injeera* bread**

Dandelion coffee

Sweet *hembesha* bread with wild seeds

Yarrow *Tej*

Yarrow
Achillea millefolium

Fat Hen
Chenopodium album

Wild food in February

Yarrow
What it looks like: Long, narrow, feathery leaves on the ground in winter, growing to 50cm tall in summer. In June and July when the plant is tall, creamy, pink-tinged flowers appear.
How it can be useful: Yarrow is used for colds and to reduce fevers. It is applied to the skin to stop bleeding. In folklore, the Greek warrior Achilles used yarrow to heal battle wounds, which is the reason for its latin name. Warning: Yarrow is best avoided if you are pregnant or breastfeeding.

Fat hen
What it looks like: It has wide, toothed leaves. Rich, mid-olive green leaves. The flowers grow on soft spikes around June. You can also use other Goosefoots, such as Good King Henry or Red goosefoot.
How it can be useful: Excellent substitute for spinach as it grows so abundantly and is easy to harvest.

Wild rocket, cabbage and mustard sprouted seeds

1 teaspoon wild rocket seeds

1 teaspoon wild cabbage seeds

1 teaspoon garlic mustard seeds

1 Place seeds you collected last Summer and Autumn in a cup of water overnight.

2 In the morning drain and place on a sprouting tray or in a clean, sterilised jam jar which has perforations in its metal lid, or has a permeable cloth secured in place (with an elastic band) over the opening.

3 Every day, drench the seeds in fresh water and drain away. Do this until seeds have sprouted. It will take between 3 and 5 days.

4 You can eat them as soon as they have sprouted or wait a few more days until they have grown more.

East African wild greens
and *injeera* bread

180g (6oz) teff flour
(or wholewheat flour)

475 ml (16fl oz) water

2 teaspoons salt

Vegetable oil

Wild greens

1 onion

1 bulb of garlic

A large handful of
yarrow, chickweed,
goosegrass, fat hen
and dandelion leaves

½ teaspoon cayenne,
cinnamon, cardamom

A pinch of nutmeg
and ground cloves

The ancient process of fermenting grains breaks down carbohydrates into a more digestible food, enhanced by friendly bacteria. Teff flour is gluten free. **Makes 8 injeera**

1 Mix the teff flour with the water and let the mixture stand in a bowl covered with a dish towel at room temperature until it bubbles and turns sour. This will take around 2 days. The fermenting mixture should be the consistency of a pancake batter. Stir in the salt.
2 Lightly oil a flat pan and put on a medium heat.
3 Pour in enough batter to cover the bottom of the pan (*injeera* bread is not supposed to be paper thin). Spread the batter around immediately by turning and rotating the pan in the air.
4 Cook until holes form in the *injeera*, the batter has become firm, and the edges lift from the pan. Don't flip it over.
5 Remove and let cool. Make more using the same process. Place cling film between breads so they don't stick together.

East African wild greens
1 Fry the onion and garlic in a little oil or clarified butter. Add the spices and continue to fry for a few minutes.
2 Chop the green leaves and add to the pot for 5 minutes.
3 Serve with *injeera* bread.

FEBRUARY

Dandelion coffee and sweet *hembesha* bread with wild seeds

6 – 8 small dandelion roots

One safe strategy for collecting your dandelion root is to go to the local allotments and ask allotment holders if you can gather their dandelions.
They'll probably love you for it. It's not easy digging up dandelions, especially the bigger ones but I content myself with digging up lots of little ones that are easier to pull out. Keep the whole plant. Dry leaves for tea or add them fresh to salads.

Coffee originated in East Africa and the coffee ceremony there is an important cultural event. Dandelion coffee also deserves a ceremony worthy of its wonderful health giving properties. It's full of the stuff your liver needs to recover from alcohol, cancer, hepatitis or plain old city stress. Dandelion root coffee can really support you to drink less caffeine. It's also high in iron, manganese, phosphorus, protein and vitamin A.

1 Clean the roots and leave to dry for a few days.
2 Chop up into small pieces. Place in the oven on a low heat for a couple of hours to fully dry and roast them at the same time.
3 Grind the roots and use in a coffee percolator. Alternatively, you can boil the roots for around 15 minutes.

The coffee ceremony is a long, slow event. Segen Ghebrekidan described it as "our version of going to the pub. It's where we sit and talk." Before serving the first batch, the aroma of coffee is wafted over the drinkers like incense.

300ml (10fl oz) lukewarm water

25g (1oz) fresh yeast

1 teaspoon ground fennel seeds

1 teaspoon ground hogweed seeds

1 teaspoon ground goosegrass seeds

1 teaspoon salt

1 egg

1 tablespoon oil

225g (8oz) plain flour

225g (8oz) wholewheat flour

The traditional seeds for this bread are fenugreek, coriander and cardamom. Use these or substitute as below.

1 Dissolve yeast in the warm water and set aside for 5 minutes.
2 Mix the eggs, oil and spices and beat lightly.
3 Sift the flour into a bowl, add the egg mixture and the yeast. Mix well and then knead for 10 minutes on a floured surface. Place dough in a clean bowl, cover and allow to rise in a warm place for at least an hour.
4 Knead dough again for 10 minutes. Place on a greased baking tray. Allow to rise in a warm place until it has doubled in size.
5 Preheat oven to 180°C (350°F/Gas Mark 4).
6 Decorate the top using a knife and bake for 30 minutes.
7 Cut into wedges and serve warm with a coffee.

FEBRUARY

Yarrow *Tej*

950ml (30fl oz) honey
2.8l (90fl oz) water
1 cup yarrow leaves

Tej is the Ethiopian and Eritrean name for mead or honey wine. This is probably the most ancient fermented drink known on the planet, originally discovered by chance as a bubbling liquid in a hollow of a tree where honey had mixed with water and begun to ferment. It's usually made with *gesho*, which is the shiny-leaf buckthorn, only found in East Africa. We're going to make *Tej* with yarrow, as it is abundant in February and has traditionally been used as an alcoholic drink on this island.

1 Mix the honey with the water and put in a sterilised large glass container with a lid or airlock. Let this stand for 2 days at room temperature.
2 Place the leaves in a small pan with enough of the honey and water mixture to cover. Bring to a boil and simmer for 20 minutes over a low heat.
3 Strain the leaves out through a clean muslin cloth.
4 Pour the boiled mixture back into the container of mixed honey and water and let it stand for an additional 7 days at room temperature.
5 Give it a stir and let it stand for another 7 days.
6 Serve either at room temperature or chilled.

Flexibility and abundance

"*We need flexibility of structure to allow in surprise and the unexpected.*

One February feast, Segen Ghebrekidan introduced people on the walk to an East African coffee ceremony. Even if people were surprised, no one batted an eyelid that they were coming on a wild food walk and there we were participating in a ceremony from the Horn of Africa. Somehow it fitted.

By saying yes to people and the resources they bring, we create a deeper sense of interconnectedness, belonging and abundance.

East Asia

Recipes from China, Japan and Korea

**Seven herb porridge –
'*Nana-kusa-gayu*'**

Nettle and burdock root *kimchi*

**Sautéed burdock root with
shepherd's purse sprinkle**

East Asian spring greens

***Jiaozi* dumplings with nettle
and garlic mustard**

***Dorayaki* pancakes with
Japanese knotweed**

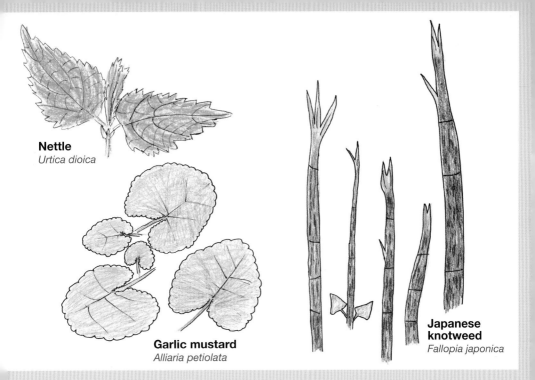

Nettle
Urtica dioica

Garlic mustard
Alliaria petiolata

Japanese knotweed
Fallopia japonica

Wild food in March

Nettle:
What it looks like: Stem and leaves are covered with hairs that are tiny needles made of silica, histamine, serotonin and formic acid, which cause the stinging.
How it can be useful: Nettle is high in calcium, iron, magnesium, vitamins A, B complex, C, D and K. It can restore the adrenal gland and relieve allergies. Use for tea, soups, stews and stirfries.

Garlic mustard
What it looks like: It has large, heart-shaped and toothed leaves, small white flowers and large seed pods. A bitter, garlic taste.
How it can be used: Eat leaves before the plant flowers as they get very bitter as the plant gets older. Steam, stir-fry, and shred raw for salads.

Japanese knotweed
What it looks like:
Heart-shaped leaves and new shoots with a reddish tinge.
How it can be useful: Don't eat Japanese knotweed anywhere in an area where you have no knowledge of land management. If you can be assured that it's free from herbicide, you could solve the problem of it spreading by eating it. With the addition of sugar, it is much like rhubarb when pureed. You can also steam the shoots as a spring vegetable.

Seven herb porridge
'Nana-kusa-gayu'

This is a Japanese dish for New Year to bring in good health and prosperity. We're making it in March around the time of the Spring Equinox.

The wonderful thing about *Nana-kusa-gayu* is that most of the traditional herbs, Japanese water dropwort, shepherd's purse, cudweed, chickweed, nipplewort, turnip greens and radish greens, are available in the UK, although we have to substitute the water dropwort.

The Japanese water dropwort *(Oenanthe javanica)* isn't toxic but our wild growing hemlock water dropwort *(Oenanthe crocata)* is lethal. If you wanted to substitute with a plant of the same family, then try cow parsley. However, it's very easy to confuse cow parsley with hemlock water dropwort, so I prefer to use what's abundant and easily available. In the original dish, the herbs are also often substituted for what's available at a dark and wintery time of year.

Our dish was made with shepherd's purse, chickweed, hedge bedstraw, dandelion, salad burnet, clover leaves, and dock leaf.

We foraged in the nature garden of Myatt's Fields Park, tasting the plants as we found them. This is Miley trying goosegrass.

225g (8oz) Japanese rice

1.5l (48fl oz) water

1 teaspoon shredded ginger

2 teaspoons salt

the 7 herbs; shepherd's purse, chickweed, hedge bedstraw, dandelion, salad burnet, clover leaves, and dock leaf

Nana-kusa-gayu is a type of rice porridge common to many Asian-influenced countries. It is a rice soup with additions of ginger, spring onion, chicken and common herbs. It is also called *kanji* (Tamil), *juk (*Cantonese, Korean)*, cháo* (Vietnamese), *chok* (Thai), *jaou (*Bengali), *zhou* (Mandarin) and *canja* (Portuguese). All these words mean gruel or broth.

1 Wash the rice. Add water to the rice and bring to the boil. Reduce the heat and simmer for 25–30 minutes until the rice is cooked. Add the herbs shortly before the rice is cooked.
2 Take the shepherd's purse seeds off the stem and lightly toast. Sprinkle a few shepherd's purse seeds on each serving.

Our seven herbs from right; dock leaf, chickweed, shepherd's purse, hedge bedstraw, salad burnet, dandelion leaf, clover leaf

Nettle and burdock root *kimchi*

Good quality sea salt

2 large handfuls
of nettle tops

A couple of small
burdock roots

1 onion

4 cloves garlic

4 chillies, any style

2 tablespoons
grated ginger

Fermenting vegetables is another common practice throughout various cultures. When you ferment vegetables you encourage the very healthy bacteria that your body needs to thrive. Salt is a key ingredient here to preserve the vegetables from microorganisms that cause decay, while also creating new nutrients, specifically the B vitamins.

A classic kimchi is made from cabbage. You could use wild cabbage, a plantain or nettle. It's the chilli and ginger that differentiate kimchi from sauerkraut, and chilli works well with both nettle and burdock. Burdock root can be dug up early in the second year of its two year span before it sends all its goodness up into creating new life above ground. Turnips or radishes can be substituted for burdock.

1 Blanch the nettles for 1 minute in boiling water, then remove and chop into small pieces.
2 Prepare the spice mix first. Grate the ginger and garlic, and chop the chilli. Chop onion finely. Mash the spices into a paste.
3 Mix 1l (1.75 pints) water and 4 tablespoons sea salt. Wash, peel and slice the burdock into 5cm (2") thin strips. Mix vegetables with the spice paste and stir thoroughly.
4 Place everything into a wide glass or ceramic dish. Add enough salt water to keep the vegetables submerged and place a plate on top with a weight on top of this. (Be careful not to build a dangerous tower that may topple.)
5 Leave for a few days, tasting every day. After 5-7 days, it will be tangy and you can store the kimchi in jars in the fridge.

Nettle picking tip:
Pick the top four pairs of leaves where all the goodness of the plant is stored in spring. Picking will encourage new growth, and if you cut them back completely around midsummer, you will get new growth in September.

Sautéed burdock root with shepherd's purse sprinkle

Burdock root

Vegetable oil

Tamari or soy sauce

Shepherd's purse seeds

For one person, you need a handful of smaller burdock roots. If you're lucky and you manage to remove a large one from the ground, you'll just need one. You'll also find burdock root in chinese and japanese supermarkets, where it will be called 'Gobo'.

1 Scrub the root, peel it and chop into 8cm (3") sections. Leave it to soak and soften in a pan of salt water for a few hours.
2 Chop into slim strips, 0.5cm - 1cm (around 0.25" – 0.5") thick.
3 Heat some oil and stir fry the strips for around 5 minutes. Add a little water to prevent sticking and then tamari or soy sauce and stir fry for another 5 minutes until soft.
4 While this is cooking, toast some shepherd's purse seeds to sprinkle on top when serving.

East Asian spring greens

A handful goosegrass stems

1 tablespoon oil

2 cloves garlic

1 small piece ginger, grated

4 tablespoons vegetable stock

2 tablespoons soy sauce

1 tablespoon cornflour

1 Whisk the stock, soy sauce and cornflour together first.
2 Heat the oil in a wok. Add garlic and ginger and fry for 3 minutes. Add the goosegrass and let wilt for 1 minute. Then add the stock liquid and simmer for a further 2 minutes. Don't overcook the goosegrass, you still want a slight crunch.
3 Serve with rice.

Jiaozi dumplings with nettle and garlic mustard

Dough

450g (1lb) plain flour

240ml (8fl oz) hot water

Filling

Large handful nettle or garlic mustard leaves

Small bunch wild garlic (or 3 cornered leek)

1 small onion, finely chopped

Vegetable oil

Dipping Sauce

3 tablespoons (2fl oz) soy sauce

1 teaspoon sesame oil

1 teaspoon sugar

1 teaspoon chilli sauce

The dumpling is common to many cultures. There are three ways of cooking the dumplings; pan frying, steaming or boiling. **Makes 16 dumplings**

1 Chop the nettle very finely. Heat some oil in a pan and sweat the chopped onion for 5 minutes. Add the nettle and cook for 3-4 minutes. Then add the wild garlic for 2 minutes.

2 In a bowl, mix the flour and cup of hot water until a soft dough forms. Knead the dough on a lightly floured surface until smooth. Roll out the dough and using the lid of a jar, cut out circles of around 8cm (3") diameter.

3 Place 1 tablespoon of filling in the centre of the circle. Lift up the edges and pinch 5 pleats to the joined edges of the dumpling to create a closed pouch. Seal tightly, otherwise the dumpling will burst open. Mix the dipping sauce ingredients in a bowl.

4 To pan fry: heat a nonstick pan until very hot. Add 1 table-spoon vegetable oil, tilting the pan to coat the sides. Fill the pan with dumplings in a single layer and fry for 2 minutes, or until the bottoms are golden brown. Now add ½ cup of water and a lid, and cook the dumplings for 7-10 minutes, until the water is absorbed. Repeat with remaining dumplings.

5 To steam: Grease a large bamboo steamer or a sieve to prevent sticking. Place dumplings in the steamer, and place over a pan of simmering water. Steam, covered, for 15 minutes.

6 To boil: Place around 5-7 dumplings in a large pan of boiling water. Simmer for 10 minutes. Serve with the dipping sauce.

Dorayaki pancakes with Japanese knotweed sauce

10 Japanese knotweed shoots

25g (1oz) sugar

5-6 tablespoons water

Pancakes

150g (6oz) self raising flour

½ teaspoon baking powder

2 eggs

75g (3oz) caster sugar

1 tablespoon honey

1 tablespoon mirin

2-3 tablespoons water

2 tablespoons sunflower oil

1 cup Japanese knotweed sauce

These pancakes are usually glued together with *anko (aduki bean paste)*, but sometimes chestnut puree is used and you could use that in the Autumn. These pancakes are a bit like Scotch pancakes (UK), pikelets (Aus and NZ) or silver dollar pancakes (Canada and US). **Makes 12 pancakes**

1 To make the knotweed sauce, chop young shoots into small sections of 2cm (1"). In a pan, heat with a little water to soften and turn to a puree.
2 Add the sugar or honey and stir to dissolve. Set aside to cool.
3 To make the pancakes, sift flour and baking powder together.
4 Whisk the eggs in a small bowl. Add the sugar, honey, oil and mirin to the eggs. Add the flour slowly and whisk until smooth.
5 Add the water slowly to make a smooth, thick batter.
6 Cover the batter and put in the fridge for 15 minutes.
7 Heat oil in a frying pan on a medium heat. Add a spoonful of batter to create a round pancake 7-8 cm (3") in diameter. Cook until dimples start appearing, and flip the pancake. Cook for a further 2 minutes.
8 Cook all the pancakes in this way, one at a time. When cool, sandwich 2 pancakes together by spreading a spoonful of knotweed sauce and some woodruff cream on one pancake (see recipe from April).

Learning

“ *This project exists because I wanted to learn about plants. I created a space for learning and invited other people along. I'm not a botanist and I'm not even a particularly great cook but I followed my urge to learn and question, and didn't allow things like not knowing, or not having a teacher, to get in the way. People came and kept coming on the walks, and the project grew and gained its own energy.*

We have a need to learn new skills and new ways of communicating with each other. Being open, humble, and honest when we don't know really helps.

Very often we don't need teachers, our curiosity just needs some company. ”

APRIL

UK and Ireland

Recipes from England, Wales, Scotland and Ireland

Welsh wild leek soup

Wild herb Glamorgan sausages and garlic mustard colcannon

Dandelion and burdock drink

Nettle haggis

Dock pudding

Pickled thistle stems

Japanese knotweed crumble and sweet woodruff cream

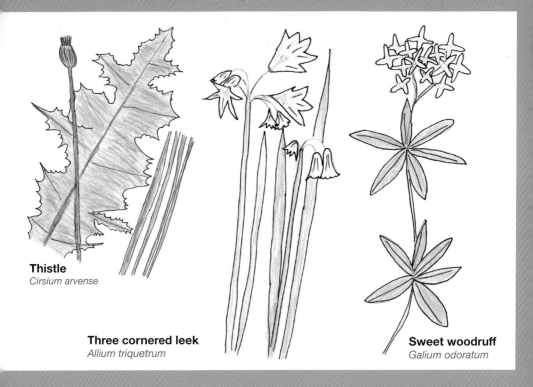

Thistle
Cirsium arvense

Three cornered leek
Allium triquetrum

Sweet woodruff
Galium odoratum

Wild food in April

Thistle
What it looks like: Long, tapered leaves with spines on wavy, toothed edges. Grows up to 1m.
How it can be useful: Shoots can be steamed or sautéed, stems can be pickled, roots can be stir-fried. Seeds can be toasted and added to salads.

Three cornered leek
What it looks like: Easy to identify three-angled stem, drooping, long-stalked white flowers with a green stripe on the outside.
How it can be useful: Make pesto, use in stir fries and salads. Don't overcook. The flowers make a beautiful garnish.

Sweet woodruff
What it looks like: Woodruff has a thin, square stem and whorls of 4-12 long, oval leaves and clusters of white flowers in June.
How it can be useful: The dried and heated plant has a vanilla fragrance which it can impart to creams and custards. Try it as a tea infusion.

Welsh wild leek soup

A large tub of wild garlic leaves and/or three cornered leek leaves

Olive oil

A large handful of chickweed

1.1l (2 pints) vegetable stock

Three cornered leek flowers for garnish

If you don't have enough of the garlic or leek leaves, add some chickweed which will give you a bright green colour and a fresh taste that will complement the strong tasting leaves.

Serves 4

1 Wash the leaves. Heat the oil in a large pan, add the leaves and cook until softened.

2 Add the stock and bring to the boil. Simmer for 3-4 minutes. Don't overcook.

3 Liquidise and serve garnished with the flowers.

Wild herb Glamorgan sausages and garlic mustard colcannon

A handful of wild garlic leaves

A handful of nettle or garlic mustard leaves

olive oil

140g (5oz) caerphilly cheese, grated

140g (5oz) breadcrumbs

2 tablespoons salad burnet, finely chopped

½ teaspoon mustard

1 egg

Colcannon

1 kg (2.2lbs) potatoes

A handful of garlic mustard leaves

50g (2oz) butter

150ml (5fl oz) double cream

Salt and pepper

A traditional vegetarian sausage dish from Wales. You can also use horseradish leaves in the Irish Colcannon dish.

1 Heat the oil. Chop the nettle and wild garlic and add to the pan. Fry until soft. Mix all the remaining ingredients together in a bowl and add the softened leaves. Shape into sausages and chill for 30 minutes in the fridge.

2 Preheat oven to 180°C (350°F/Gas Mark 4). Grease a tray, place sausages on tray and brush with oil.

3 Cook for 20 minutes, turning halfway through.

4 Meanwhile, bring potatoes to the boil in a pan of cold water and simmer until soft.

5 Melt half the butter in a frying pan, and fry the garlic mustard for 5 minutes. Take off the heat.

6 Drain potatoes in a colander and mash until smooth.

7 Heat the cream with remaining butter and beat this into the potato.

8 Add garlic mustard to the mix. Season with salt and pepper.

9 Serve with the sausages and some sautéed thistle stems.

APRIL

Dandelion and burdock drink

*600ml (21fl oz/1 pint)
cold water*

1 teaspoon burdock root

*1 teaspoon
dandelion root*

2cm (1") piece ginger

1 whole star anise

*½ teaspoon citric acid
(optional)*

*300g (10.5oz)
granulated sugar*

Sparkling water to serve

1 Chop the roots into small pieces and boil with the spices for 20 minutes. Remove from the heat and add the sugar, stirring while it dissolves.

2 Leave to cool. Add citric acid to help preserve the drink for longer, and bottle in sterilised bottles.

3 Dilute with sparkling water to serve.

Nettle haggis

Large tub of nettle tops

Large handful of wild garlic

1 carrot

4-5 mushrooms

75g (3oz) red lentils

250ml (9fl oz) vegetable stock (for lentils)

400g (14oz) tin of your favourite bean (eg kidney, borlotti, cannellini)

50g (2oz) rolled oats

50g (2oz) pot barley, soaked overnight

200ml (7fl oz) vegetable stock (for barley)

25g (1 oz) walnuts

1 teaspoon soy sauce

1 teaspoon Worcestershire sauce

2 tablespoons lemon juice

Haggis is a Scottish dish, traditionally using sheep's heart, liver and lungs. This is a vegetarian version and can be served in bite-sized chunks as an unusual canapé.

1 Preheat the oven to 180°C (350°F/Gas Mark 4).
2 Cook the pot barley in 200ml stock for around 40 minutes.
3 Cook the lentils in 250ml stock for around 15 minutes.
4 In a large frying pan, add oil and sweat the grated carrot and chopped mushrooms for 10 minutes. Add the chopped nettle tops for another 4-5 minutes. Add the cooked lentils, barley, beans and walnuts to the vegetable mixture.
5 Gently toast the rolled oats for a few minutes, and add to the mixture with the soy sauce and lemon juice.
6 Simmer for a few minutes until the liquid begins to disappear.
7 Turn into a greased ovenproof dish and cook for 30 minutes.
8 Serve with the colcannon or cut into bite-sized pieces for an unusual canapé.

Dock pudding

A large handful bistort leaves

6 large blackcurrant leaves

A small handful wild garlic leaves

150g (6oz) oatmeal

75g (3oz) whole grain or pot barley

1 teaspoon sea salt

Butter or oil for frying

This pudding comes from Yorkshire and Cumbria in the north of England. There are different kinds of barley; pearl barley is the most refined and quickest to cook, then there is pot barley which is less processed and more nutritious and then whole grain (or dehulled) barley, with just the hull removed. If you can't find bistort or are unsure about identifying it, use nettles, or curled dock, which is the most common of all docks. **Serves 4**

1 Wash the bistort leaves, blackcurrant leaves and garlic leaves. Chop very finely.
2 Add the herbs to a bowl along with the oatmeal, barley and salt. Add enough water to the bowl so that the ingredients are entirely covered. Drape a cloth over the top and leave overnight.
3 In the morning, grease a round pudding basin and transfer the mixture to it. Steam the pudding in a large saucepan so the water comes about half way up the pudding basin. Place a square of tin foil padding at the bottom of the saucepan so the basin isn't touching the bottom of the pan, as it could crack. Put a lid on the saucepan and check regularly so the water doesn't evaporate. Steam in this way for 1 hour. Allow to cool.
4 Turn out when cool and cut into 2cm (1") slices. Fry these slices in butter and serve immediately.

Pickled thistle stems

Enough thistle stems to fill 2 medium jars

1 teaspoon sea salt

300ml (10fl oz) cider vinegar

200g (8oz) soft brown sugar

3 cloves garlic

½ teaspoon celery seeds

½ teaspoon mustard seeds

After picking, thistle stems will wilt after about 30 minutes so be prepared to make the pickle straight away.

1 Add the vinegar, sugar, garlic and seeds to a pan and bring to the boil. Turn off the heat.
2 While this mixture is cooling slightly, prepare the thistles. It's the inner vegetable of thistles you want. Remove the outer stringy skin. This will peel off quite easily to leave a hollow stem. Run water through the hollow 'straw' to clean the inside.
3 Chop into sticks to fit the jars. Ladle pickling liquid into the jar, covering the stems but not right to the top of the jar. Close with non-metallic lids and label.
4 Leave for 1 month to mature. Keep in the fridge after opening.

Japanese knotweed crumble and sweet woodruff cream

200g (8oz) plain flour

150g (6oz) brown sugar

200g (7oz) unsalted butter

20 Japanese knotweed shoots

50g (2oz) granulated sugar or

3 tablespoons honey

10 tablespoons water

Cream

450ml (16fl oz) double cream

3 egg yolks

10 sprigs sweet woodruff

50g (2oz) caster sugar

Japanese knotweed cooked in this way has the texture of rhubarb. Only use Japanese knotweed if you have a reliable source (see note in March). Sweet woodruff doesn't have much of a flavour when fresh, but when it's dried or cooked it develops a vanilla honey flavour.

1 Preheat the oven to 180°C (350F/Gas Mark 4).
2 Add the sugar to the flour. Cube the butter and crumble it into the flour until there are no lumps of butter left.
3 Chop the knotweed shoots into small sections. Place in a pan with the water. Heat gently and allow to soften and turn to a puree. Add the sugar and stir to dissolve.
4 Place the knotweed mixture in a baking dish. Place the crumble mixture on top and bake for 20 minutes.
5 Put the woodruff in a saucepan with the cream and bring to the boil. Leave to infuse for 15 minutes. Remove the woodruff.
6 Whisk the egg yolks and the sugar. Add to the infused cream and gently heat until the sugar has dissolved. Simmer for 10 minutes, stirring constantly or until the cream thickens and will coat the back of a wooden spoon.
7 Pour into a bowl to cool and then serve with the hot crumble.

Persistence

" *While writing this book, I got stuck when I started to believe that the world is too competitive and cut-throat for a project of experiments into how plants and food can build community. This disconnected me from my trust that connection to each other and to nature matters.*

I had to keep coming back to my original intention for connection, and my love of the new and unexpected, and then I could find the energy to keep going. "

Central and Eastern Europe

Recipes from Poland, Germany, Romania and Bulgaria

Wild cabbage *sauerkraut*

Curled dock pie – '*Vărzar cu dragavei*'

Nettle and thistle *pierogi*

Elderflower fritters

Elderflower and strawberry jam

Wild sorrel soup and eggs

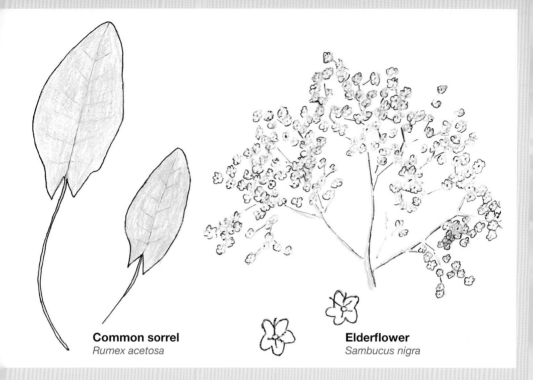

Common sorrel
Rumex acetosa

Elderflower
Sambucus nigra

Wild food in May

Common sorrel

What it looks like: Leaves are shaped like arrows with tapered points and two lobes at the bottom, where the leaf joins the stem. It has a lemon taste - a little nibble will help to identify.

How it can be useful: The tart, lemon flavour of the leaves make them a useful addition to salads and as a substitute for lemon in dressings. Sorrel contains oxalic acid, which can be toxic in large quantities, so don't overeat and don't eat at all if at risk of kidney stones.

Elderflower

What it looks like: Look out for the gnarled, twisting trunk of the tree which grows to around 10m. Flowers appear at the end of April in London and stay on the tree until June. The blossoms are hundreds of tiny, creamy flowerlets arranged in clusters. Tiny round black berries appear in August and September. Don't overpick the flowers otherwise there won't be any berries!

How it can be useful: Use in jam together with other early summer fruit, or as a fritter. The flower infusion is beneficial for colds, catarrh, hayfever and is a calming night-time drink.

Wild cabbage *sauerkraut*

A large handful of young wild cabbage leaves

Sea salt

¼ teaspoon caraway seeds, dill seeds, celery seeds or juniper berries

Glass or ceramic wide-mouthed container

Plate that fits into the mouth of the container

There are good reasons to ferment food; the process creates beneficial bacteria in the digestive system, which help you absorb food better. Fermenting foods also helps preserve them without losing any nutrients. You can spend a fortune on 'healthy' food products but fermenting them yourself is simple and very economical. This makes a very earthy *sauerkraut,* which is itself a great stuffing for *pierogi.*

1 Chop the leaves finely. Sprinkle salt on the leaves. The salt pulls water out of the leaves (through osmosis), and this creates the brine in which the leaf can ferment and sour without rotting.
2 Add the spices. Mix all the ingredients together and pack into a glass jar tightly to force water out of the vegetables. Cover with a plate or some other lid that fits snugly inside the jar.
3 Place a clean, heavy weight on the plate. This weight is to force water out of the vegetables and keep them submerged. Cover with a cloth to keep dust and flies out. Press down on weight to add pressure and help force water out. If the *sauerkraut* isn't submerged in the brine by the following morning, add some more salt water.
4 Check the *sauerkraut* every day or two. Sometimes mould appears on the surface and you can skim it off. The *sauerkraut* itself is protected by the brine. Generally, it becomes tangy and is ready after a few days.

Curled dock pie – 'Vărzar cu dragavei'

500g (20oz) plain flour

100g (4oz)
softened butter

25g (1oz) yeast

1 egg

4 tablespoons (3fl oz)
lukewarm water

1 teaspoon salt

Filling

A large bag of curled
dock

50g (2oz) dill

400g (14oz) telemea
cheese (or substitute
feta cheese)

3 eggs

This Romanian dish is usually made with mountain spinach. Here the filling is curled dock.   **Serves 4**

1 Preheat oven to 180°C (350°F/Gas Mark 4).
2 Dissolve the yeast in the lukewarm water and leave aside for a few minutes.
3 To make the dough: mix the butter, cubed into small pieces, with the flour and salt. Add the egg and the yeast mixture. Work all the ingredients together with your hands. When the dough stops sticking to the bowl, it's ready.
4 Chop the curled dock and the dill finely. Crumble the cheese and add to the dock and dill. Then add the eggs, and mix well.
5 Roll the dough out to 0.5cm thick, and line a greased baking tray with it. Add the curled dock mix, spreading it evenly. Roll out the remaining dough, and place it on top of the curled dock mix.
6 Place in the oven and bake for 40-50 minutes until the crust becomes golden.
7 Serve with *sauerkraut* or another pickle.

Nettle and thistle *pierogi*

20 thistle shoots
(outer skin removed)

20 nettle tops

A small bunch wild
garlic

1 onion, chopped

Salad burnet to garnish

Oil for frying

Pierogi dough

450g (1lb) plain flour

2 eggs, beaten

½ teaspoon salt

90ml (3fl oz) water

30ml (1fl oz) sour cream
(or substitute with the
same amount of water)

Pierogi are a Polish version of a common dish throughout the world; stuffed dumplings, which are then boiled, steamed or fried. The Jewish version are called *kreplach,* the Chinese version are called *jiaozi,* the Italians call them *ravioli,* in Japan, they are *gyoza* and in Nepal, they are called *momo.* Everyone loves a stuffed dumpling! The Polish version includes sour cream in the dough. **Makes 20 *pierogi***

1 Fry the onion in oil until translucent. Add the nettles, thistles and wild garlic, all chopped roughly, and sauté for 5 minutes. Season well.
2 Mix the eggs, water and sour cream together in a bowl.
3 In another bowl, mix the flour and the salt. Add the egg mixture to the flour mixture. Work the ingredients together with your hands to make a smooth dough. If the dough is too sticky to roll easily, add a bit more flour. If the dough is too dry, add a bit more water.

Myatt's Fields Park nature garden had a problem with thistles so we decided to eat them as a stuffing for pierogi. You need gloves for the job, and a lot of help!

4 On a lightly floured working surface, knead the dough until it is smooth and stretches without tearing.

5 To assemble and cook: Roll out so the dough is 5mm (0.2") thick. Cut 8cm (3") diameter circles. Add a small amount of the nettle filling to the top half of each circle. Bring the bottom edge up to meet the top edge and pinch seams together so the top resembles a wavy fan. Ensure seams are well sealed.

6 Bring a pan of water to the boil. Add 3–4 pierogi at a time. Boil for 5 minutes. Remove one by one with a slotted spoon.

7 You can eat straight away or fry in butter to make them crispy. Fresh salad burnet leaves make an attractive garnish.

Aleksandra Magdziarek showed us how to make the pastry and stuff the pierogi, which we did outside on a wooden board. Many hands making light work.

Elderflower fritters

16 heads of elderflower

1 egg

225ml (8fl oz) ice cold water

140g (5 oz) plain flour

1 pinch salt

1l (1.75pt) vegetable oil for frying

Icing sugar, sieved

2 lemons, cut into wedges

The elderflower fritter is one of the most joyful foods ever. Coming together to eat elderflower fritters is a wonderful reason for a party. This is community feasting at its best! Have your serving arrangements all set out so people can eat as the frying happens. Have a plate with lemon segments and another with icing sugar that people can dip into with their fritter. The elderflower head stem is a superb handle both for frying and then eating. Take turns frying so the frier doesn't miss out. **Makes 16 fritters**

1 Make the batter first by beating the egg, then adding the water, continuing to beat the mixture as you do so. Slowly sift the flour and salt into the egg and water mixture, whisking to make sure there are no lumps.

2 Heat the oil in a pan until almost at smoking point. Dip the elderflower heads in the batter, then remove and let the excess batter drip off before you put the battered fritter into the oil. Hold it by the stem and be careful of spitting oil. Fry for 15 seconds or until golden brown. Keep your eye on the game. Drain on absorbent paper.

3 Serve immediately. Squeeze lemon juice on the fritters and dip them in icing sugar.

Elderflower and strawberry jam

1.5 kg (3lb) strawberries

1.5kg (3lb) jam sugar (with added pectin)

Juice of 1 lemon

2 heads of elderflowers (flowers stripped from stalks)

When I made this delicious jam with a group of children they were shocked how much sugar went in, but were delighted by the taste. **Makes 3 jars**

1 Put the strawberries, sugar and lemon juice in a heavy-bottomed pan. Place the pan over a gentle heat and stir until the sugar dissolves. This must be done slowly to avoid burning. When all the sugar is dissolved, raise the heat and boil rapidly for around 10-15 minutes. Towards the end of this time, add the elderflowers torn off their stems and stir briefly before doing the jam setting test.

2 To test if the jam will set: put a teaspoon of the mixture on a chilled saucer and run your finger through it. If it wrinkles, it's ready. If it's still runny, boil for another 5 minutes and try the test again. Don't be tempted to overboil your jam.

3 Pour into sterilised jars and seal. It will keep for up to a year, but won't last this long with hungry children around.

Elderflower & Strawberry Jam 2011

Wild sorrel soup and eggs

1 large bagful of fresh sorrel leaves

1l (34fl oz) vegetable stock

2 medium potatoes

3 tablespoons (2fl oz) sour cream

1 teaspoon salt

4 eggs

3 leaves dill or sorrel to garnish

Sorrel as a soup ingredient is common across Eastern Europe. In Romania, sorrel is known as *măcris.* In Russia and Ukraine, it is called *shchavel* and the soup made with it is called *shav.* In Hungary, it is called *sóska* and in Poland, *szczaw.*   **Serves 4**

1 Chop the potatoes into small pieces. Add to the pan of stock and bring to the boil. Simmer for 10 minutes.

2 Add the sorrel leaves to the pan and cook for 2 minutes. Then liquidise the mixture and stir in the sour cream.

3 Hard boil the eggs for around 7-10 minutes, depending on how hard you like them.

4 To serve, chop the eggs in half and add to a bowl of soup. Sprinkle with leaves to garnish.

Flow

“ *The monthly feasts became large events for around 50 people. Each feast incorporated many activities. For example when we made pierogi in the park, we harvested the thistle shoots from the nature garden (we decided to eat them to control them), we made the dough, prepared the shoots, stuffed the pierogi and ate them. There were books of East European folktales if you fancied listening to a story. The aim was to flow between many integrated strands of activities rather than segregate them into separate events.*

Principles of Open Space are very useful to support the flow of an event; 1) whoever comes are the right people to come, 2) whenever it starts is the right time to start, 3) whatever happens is the only thing that could have happened, and 4) when it's over, it's over. ”

West Africa

Recipes from Nigeria, Sierra Leone and Ghana

Akara balls and nasturtium *ata* sauce

Braised wild cabbage and plantain leaves

Nettle and peanut stew

West African mallow stew with *fufu*

Mallow *jollof* rice

Nettle and ginger beer

Common mallow
Malva sylvestris

Nasturtium
Tropaeolum majus

Wild food in June

Common mallow
What it looks like: Grows up to 90cm. Leaves are palmately-lobed. Pinky-purple flowers appear in June. Avoid any diseased plants with orange spot rust. The word mallow is derived from the old English *malwe*, which means soft.

How it can be useful: Mallow contains vitamin A and is high in protein. It is one of the oldest medicinal plants in the world. The leaves are very high in mucilage, which can help soften the skin. I always use mallow for sore throats and find it more effective than sage.

Nasturtium
What it looks like: It has rounded (or shield-shaped) leaves with the stalk on the underside of the centre of the leaf. The flowers have five or more petals and a funnel-shaped nectar tube at the back. It's not really a wild food but it self seeds easily in pots. It is native to South America and contains a peppery oil similar to that in watercress.

How it can be useful: Flowers and leaves are great in a salad or use the larger leaves to roll into cigar shapes stuffed with rice. Collect the seeds to plant next year, or grind them and use as black pepper which is what people did during wartime in the 1940s. The beautiful nasturtium brightens up a grey city.

Akara balls and nasturtium *ata* sauce

A large handful of nasturtium leaves and flowers

A smaller handful of dandelion leaves

1 onion

2 tablespoons palm oil

5-6 tomatoes

1 scotch bonnet pepper

Akara balls

225g (½lb) dried black-eyed peas

1 large onion

1 scotch bonnet pepper

Salt and pepper

Oil for frying

This is another great dish for community feasting and is very satisfying to prepare and to eat together. It doesn't work with tinned black-eyed peas as you can't get the skins off, so make sure you buy dried peas. You can also buy dried peas already without their skins in African shops. Some versions of *ata* sauce include bitterleaf, for which we are substituting dandelion. You can leave out the scotch bonnet pepper and experiment with the peppery taste of the nasturtium leaves. Or have both!   Serves 8

1 First make the *ata* sauce. Roughly chop the onion and the tomatoes, then whizz together in a blender until the mixture forms a paste.

2 Heat the palm oil and add the onion and the tomatoes. Cook for 5 minutes on a low heat. Leave to cool. Chop the nasturtium and dandelion leaves very finely, and add to the cooled tomato and onion mixture. You may want to whizz this mixture again in the blender for a smoother sauce.

3 To make the *akara* balls, first prepare the beans. Soak them in warm water for 1 hour then whizz in a blender for 2-3 seconds only. Drain away the water and floating bean skins. Rub the remaining skins off between your fingers. The bean mixture now looks white and crumbly.

4 Blend the bean mixture again, now that the skins are removed, with the chopped onion, chilli and salt and pepper until milkshake smooth. The mixture should be moist but not runny.

5 Heat the oil in a pan until hot but not smoking. Add the bean mixture in dessertspoon measures. Fry until golden brown for about 4 minutes. You can fry many in one go. When golden brown, remove with a metal slotted spoon onto kitchen towel to absorb excess oil.

6 Serve by dipping into the nasturtium *ata* sauce.

Akara balls are great hot or cold with ata or other West African sauces, such as shito sauce from Ghana.

Braised wild cabbage leaves

1 large bagful of wild cabbage leaves

3 tablespoons butter

2 medium onions, thinly sliced

1 clove garlic

1 scotch bonnet pepper

2 slices fresh ginger

This is a traditional leafy dish from Southern Africa. You can use wild cabbage and also the generous leaves of greater plantain which are abundant and easy to harvest. Serves 4

1 Place the butter in a pan and heat it until it foams, taking care so it doesn't burn. Add the onion slices, crushed garlic, chilli and ginger and cook until the onion is lightly browned.
2 Chop the wild cabbage, add to the pan and cook for 10 minutes over a low heat, stirring frequently.
3 Serve with rice or *fufu*.

Nettle and peanut stew

1 large tub nettle tops, chopped roughly

1 large onion, chopped

5 medium tomatoes

1 large sweet potato, chopped

150g (5oz) peanuts

2cm piece of fresh ginger, chopped

1 scotch bonnet pepper, chopped

2 tablespoons vegetable oil

When Mary, a Nigerian friend, first tasted nettles, she begged me to show her where to find them and to cook them again as she said she felt revitalised by them.   **Serves 4**

1 Fry the onion in the oil until light golden in a frying pan. Stir in the chopped ginger, and the cinnamon stick. Then add the sweet potato, chilli, tomatoes and around 500ml water. Stir, cover and bring to the boil, then simmer for 15 minutes.

2 Grind the peanuts into small pieces. Add them to the stew with some salt and pepper, and stir. Add the nettle tops and simmer for a further 5 minutes, stirring frequently.

3 Serve with plenty of freshly ground black pepper.

West African mallow stew with *fufu*

1 large bagful
of mallow leaves

1 large yam

1 onion

1 scotch bonnet pepper

Palm oil

Dried fish (optional, go
to your local African
store for guidance on
what to buy)

Variants on the mallow are called *crain-crain* in Sierra Leone, and *ewedu* in Nigeria. They are prized for their mucilaginous properties (rather like okra) which really nourish your insides. The traditional way of making *fufu* is boiling cassava root, then pounding it. Some people put a little oil on their hands before touching raw yam as it can cause itchiness and the oil seems to prevent this.   Serves 4

1 Fry a chopped onion and the chilli in palm oil.
2 In a different saucepan, boil the chopped mallow for 10 minutes to break down the plant fibres. For a traditional flavour, add some chunks of dried fish to the mallow pan.
3 To make the *fufu*, peel the yam and cut into small pieces. Cover the yams with cold water in a pot, bring to the boil and simmer for 20 minutes or until the yams are tender. Drain the yams and let cool. Add a little oil (or butter), salt and pepper. Pound the yams into a smooth paste with a potato masher until the *fufu* becomes smooth.
4 To eat, mould the *fufu* into balls with your hands to scoop up the sauce and the greens.

Mallow *jollof* rice

20 mallow leaves

20 yarrow leaves

1 large onion, chopped

1 red pepper, chopped

1 yellow pepper, chopped

2 garlic cloves

1 x 400g can plum tomatoes

2cm piece ginger

1 scotch bonnet pepper

3 tablespoons vegetable oil

3 tablepoons tomato puree

400g (14 oz) rice

A stock cube

No cookbook coming from London would be complete without a recipe for *jollof* rice. At my son's school they have termly family feasts and I always look forward to tasting a variety of *jollof* rices! In this vegetarian version, I've added protein-rich mallow to make it a meal in itself.   Serves 6

1 Fry the onion in some oil in a pan until soft.
2 Meanwhile, whizz garlic, tomatoes, ginger and chilli in a blender until smooth. Transfer to a pan and add the tomato purée, stock cube and 600ml water. Bring to the boil, then simmer for 10 minutes.
3 Wash the rice and add to the pan. Scatter the yellow and red peppers, along with the chopped mallow and yarrow leaves. Cover and cook, for about 10 minutes, until the rice is tender.
4 Serve with chopped mallow leaves as a garnish.

Nettle and ginger beer

I made this nettle and ginger beer (which is actually a soft drink) with some children in Brixton. We picked the nettles, fermented the drink, created a label and sold it in Brixton Cornercopia in the market.   **20 small bottles**

50 nettle tops

6l (10.5 pints) water

25g (1oz) cream of tartar

750g (1.5lb) sugar

A large chunk of ginger, grated

15g (0.5 oz) yeast

1 Boil the nettle tops in the water for 10 minutes. Strain back into another saucepan. Add the cream of tartar and the sugar, and heat gently to allow the sugar to dissolve.

2 Leave until just warm, then transfer into a fermenting vat or a large clean bucket, preferably with a lid (but you can also cover with a tea towel). Add the grated ginger and the yeast to the vat, and stir well.

3 Leave covered for 4 days to ferment. Drain the beer to remove the ginger and put into bottles. Try to leave the yeast sediment in the vat.

4 Serve chilled with lemon or mint.

Play and fun

" *We feel alive and happy when we play, whether we are a child or an adult. In a community event, it's crucial to include children both for their wellbeing and for the wellbeing of adults in general, and their parents in particular.*

As the African saying goes, 'It takes a village to raise a child'. The inclusion of children in community events also has the benefit of children learning that they are part of a safe community that cares for their development.

In the feasts, both adults and children played at things like making May baskets of 10 wild plants, rolling a ball of ice cream in a container around a pond in Summer, and decorating wreaths with wild plants in Winter. We also had unstructured time, where we would go to a safe green space, and the children were free to explore and structure their own play. "

JULY

North Africa and Middle East

Recipes from Morocco, Algeria, Iran, Iraq and Egypt

Mallow soup – *'Molokhia'*

Moroccan Mallow stew –
'Khoubiza' or 'Bekkoula'

Lime flower tea

Rose petal jelly with cardamom
and almond

Goosegrass seed coffee

Mallow flower purple cake

Stuffed lime leaves and sumac dressing

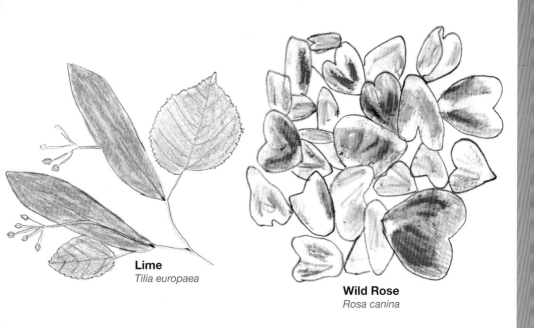

Lime
Tilia europaea

Wild Rose
Rosa canina

Wild food in July

A note on seed collecting
From now on, keep your eye open for seeds. Wild rocket and all kinds of mustard seeds (garlic mustard, field mustard etc) can be sprouted into a healthy vegetable (see February). Seeds can be toasted as a topping for soups, vegetables and bread (see February, March and October). Collect plantain seed as a thickener for stews (see December).

Lime
What it looks like: Tall tree growing up to 40m with bushy side shoots around the trunk. Leaves are heart shaped, growing into a taper, and are fine toothed. Sweet flowers appear in July, hanging from long leaf-like bracts.
How it can be useful: Leaves can be shredded and added to salads, or blanched and stuffed. The flowers make a soothing infusion which can be drunk or applied to the skin.

Wild rose
What it looks like: A common, wild rose with large flat pink flowers appearing in June and July. Stems are long and arching and covered with hooked thorns.
How it can be useful: Petals can be used fresh for jelly, or making skin lotions. You can also dry petals for tea.

Mallow soup – 'Molokhia'

2 large handfuls fresh mallow leaves

1l (1.75 pint) chicken or vegetable stock

1 carrot

1 onion

3-4 cloves garlic

1 teaspoon freshly ground coriander seeds

1 teaspoon freshly ground cumin seeds

1 teaspoon cayenne pepper

2-3 cardamom pods

Olive oil

The *Corchorus,* which is traditionally used for this dish throughout the region, is a plant in the Malvaceae or Mallow family. When mallow is cooked for a long time, it acquires the mucilaginous or 'slimy' quality that this popular dish is famous for.   **Serves 4**

1 Sweat the onion in olive oil until translucent. Grate the carrot and add to the pan for a further 5 minutes.
2 Chop the mallow leaves very finely. Add to the pan together with the hot stock. Let this cook for 15 minutes.
3 Meanwhile, fry the garlic, coriander, cumin and cardamom seeds, and the cayenne pepper for around 5 minutes.
4 Add the spice paste to the soup and serve on a bed of rice.

Moroccan Mallow stew – 'Khoubiza' or 'Bekkoula'

1 large bagful of common mallow

1 bunch coriander

4-5 cloves garlic

4-5 tomatoes

1 bird's eye chilli

2 tablespoons ground cumin

2 tablespoons sweet noble paprika

1 small jar olives

1 small tin tomato puree

This is a rich, wholesome dish with tomatoes and olives, taught to me by Aisha. If you ever find yourself using dried mallow, you'll need to double the cooking time.   Serves 4

1 Gently fry the garlic for a couple of minutes. Chop the tomatoes, add them and stir for a few minutes.
2 Add the chopped coriander, sweet noble paprika, the tomato puree and a little water.
3 Chop the mallow and add. Simmer for 10 minutes or 20 minutes if you're using dried mallow.
4 Add the olives and simmer for a further 5 minutes.

Rose petal jelly
with cardamom and almond

0.5l (1 pint) rose petals

450g (1lb) jam sugar
(with added pectin)

0.5l (1 pint) water

2 lemons

1 tablespoon almond
slivers

1 teaspoon cardamom
pods

Resist the temptation to overboil your jelly because you're worried it won't set. Better a too runny jelly that you spoon onto bread and yoghurt than an overset, rubbery jelly. You know you've reach setting point if, when you run your finger through the jelly on a cold saucer (put in a fridge first for 10 minutes), it leaves a trail.

1 Begin with enough rose petals to fill 1 pint of a measuring jug. Simmer them in the pint of water for 5 minutes.

2 Strain the liquid to remove the petals. Add the juice of 2 lemons and 450g (1lb) jam sugar. Heat gently until the sugar is dissolved. Crush the cardamom pods and add with the almond slivers. Boil for 15 minutes or until you reach setting point.

3 Put in sterilised jars, adding a few fresh petals if you like the look of the petals in the jar.

Lime flower tea

2 flower heads per cup of tea

1 Place the flower heads directly in the cup you drink from or put them in a teapot to brew for 5 minutes before serving.

Goosegrass and hogweed seed coffee

100 stems of cleavers

1 tablespoon hogweed seed

The juicy green stems of cleavers or goosegrass become dry and brown in July. Now is the time to pick the seeds for drying and roasting to make a delicious coffee substitute that also supports your lymphatic system. Go out to gather cleavers seeds with a group of friends as you need a lot!

Serves 6

1 Pick the seeds off one by one, or cut large swathes of cleavers plants and bring inside to prepare. Alternatively, if you walk through the plants in a natural fibre, the seeds will stick to your clothes.

2 The seeds may be a little moist or even a bit green so you'll need to dry and toast them on the hob in a frying pan. Slowly and attentively, on a low heat, allow the moisture to be released from the seeds which will gradually turn brown. Pay attention to not burn them.

3 Toast some hogweed seed for a delicate cardamom flavour.

4 Grind all the seeds in a pestle and mortar or in a coffee grinder. If you brew your coffee in a cafetière, you'll need a generous 2cm of grounds in the bottom of the cafetière.

5 Alternatively, you can boil the whole seeds in a saucepan with water for 10 minutes to produce an even fuller flavour.

Mallow flower purple cake

150g (6oz) flour

50g (2oz) ground hazelnuts

70g (3oz) caster sugar

120ml (4fl oz) buttermilk

25ml (1fl oz) sunflower oil

2 tablespoons poppy seeds

2 eggs

1 teaspoon baking powder

A cupful of dried mallow flowers

The mallow flowers leave a lovely purplish stain in the sponge. For a dairy-free cake, replace the eggs and the butter milk with 225ml (8fl oz) non-dairy milk, soured by whisking in a teaspoon of vinegar, and increase the oil content to 85ml (3fl oz). If you leave out the nuts, increase the flour to 200g (8oz).

1 Preheat the oven to 180°C (350°F/Gas Mark 4).
2 Add all the dry ingredients together except the flowers.
3 Add the oil to the milk and beat in the eggs.
4 Add the liquid mixture to the dry mixture.
5 Stir well, adding the flowers at the last minute.
6 Put in a greased cake tin and bake in the oven for 40 minutes. Insert a clean knife into the cake, if it comes out clean, the cake is ready.

JULY

Stuffed lime leaves and sumac dressing

20 large lime leaves

1 onion

4 cloves garlic

100g (4oz) rice

5 tablespoons olive oil

3 tablespoons lemon juice

1 tablespoon crushed sumac fruits

Salt and pepper

Make sure you pick the young, light green lime leaves. Sumac is widely planted in gardens so you might have to knock on some doors and ask to pick some. Crush the flowers to a dark red powder for the dressing in this dish.

1 Pick the larger of the young lime leaves. Wash them, then blanch them in boiling water for 1 minute. Remove from the water and leave stacked on a plate for stuffing.

2 Fry some onion and garlic for 5 minutes. Add the washed rice and 2 parts water for 1 part rice. Season generously with salt and pepper. When cooked, leave to cool.

3 Stuff the leaves by placing a small amount of rice mixture on the stalk end of the leaf placed nearest to you. Fold in the sides and then roll the leaf into a cigar shape as tightly as possible, without ripping the leaves.

4 For the dressing, mix together the olive oil, lemon juice and crushed sumac, and season with salt and pepper.

Support

" *This project functioned with a lot of support. Some of this support was very practical; sharing recipes, coming to cook or taking equipment to the park. Some was the emotional and moral support of having conversations about the project.*

The moral support was in the form of face-to-face or telephone chats where I would talk about fears that were coming up, or celebrations of tiny steps forward. The person listening to me wouldn't give advice or suggest strategies. They would reflect back to me what I was saying, so I could gain greater understanding of what was going on.

In the space created between me beginning to talk and the other person finishing reflecting back my words, there is often a shift into clarity, acceptance or greater spaciousness. "

The Caribbean

Recipes from Jamaica, Barbados, Trinidad and Tobago

Wild herb Jamaican patties

Nettle, saltfish and boiled dumplings

Ash key pickle

Blackberry ice cream

Blackberry Irish moss smoothie

Yellow rice and elderberries

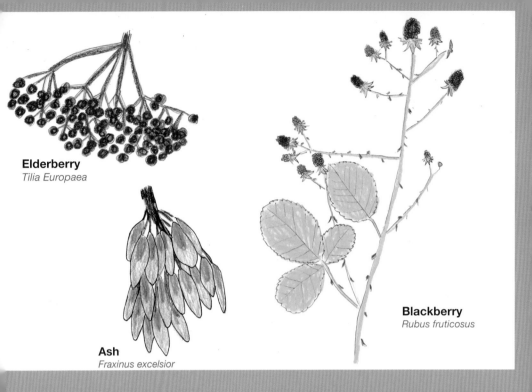

Elderberry
Tilia Europaea

Ash
Fraxinus excelsior

Blackberry
Rubus fruticosus

Wild food in August

Elderberry
What it looks like: The tree has a gnarled, twisting trunk. Clusters of berries in bunches appear in early August.
How it can be useful: This is *the* fruit to use to boost the immune system, to protect from colds, flu and viruses. Make tincture, cordial, jelly and chutney with it. Freezing elderberries rather than drying them is the more reliable way of storing them.

Ash
What it looks like: The ash has leaves with around 10 long-tipped leaflets and is distinguishable by the black terminal bud, shaped like a bishop's mitre at the end of the branches. The ash key is the long-winged fruit that appears in Summer.
How it can be useful: Pickle the keys to make an interesting aperitif with a glass of cold beer.

Blackberry
What it looks like: Leaves have 3-5 leaflets and prickles all along the stems. White or light pink flowers appear in May, and the fruit starts to appear in July.
How it can be useful: Eat them fresh or take home for jam, ice cream and pies. They are high in vitamin C and antioxidants to protect cells.

Wild herb Jamaican patties

1 large handful of wild herbs (nettle, dandelion, bittercress, chickweed, yarrow)

1 onion

3-4 cloves garlic

2cm piece fresh root ginger

4-5 tomatoes

1 scotch bonnet pepper

Pastry

280g (10oz) flour

½ teaspoon salt

200g (7oz) goat's butter

240ml (8fl oz) cold water

1 teaspoon ground turmeric

1 teaspoon cayenne pepper

Melted coconut oil

Many cultural influences contributed to the development of the patty; the English pasty, Indian curry seasonings, the scotch bonnet pepper and annatto seeds from the Americas, and cayenne pepper from Africa. The classic patty crust is yellow from the addition of turmeric or annatto seeds. The soft, flaky pastry is often made with goat's fat and I'm choosing to use a slightly salty goat's butter here. The patty is a wonderful 'street food' and certainly my choice, when I do my errands around Brixton.   **Makes 10 patties**

1 First cook the filling. Fry the onion and garlic in oil and add the finely chopped ginger. Cook for 3 minutes.

If the dough is too dry, add a little water. Use any round shape of approximately 10cm in diameter to cut out the circles. Seal together with a fork.

2 Finely chop the tomatoes and the scotch bonnet pepper, and add to the pan, stirring and cooking for a further 5 minutes.

3 Add the selection of wild herbs, finely chopped and cook for 5 minutes. Set aside.

4 Preheat the oven to 180°C (350°F/Gas Mark 4). Sift together the flour, turmeric and salt into a bowl.

5 Cube the butter then add to the flour mix and rub in with your fingertips until the mixture resembles fine crumbs.

6 Add just enough water to bind the mixture as a firm dough. Turn onto a lightly-floured surface and knead for a few minutes until smooth.

7 Roll the dough out to 4mm (0.15") thick then cut into circles about 10cm (4") in diameter.

8 Fill with wild herb filling then fold into half-moon shapes, seal, glaze with melted coconut oil, then bake in the oven for about 20 minutes, or until golden.

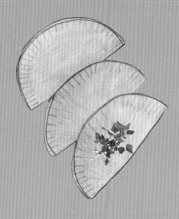

AUGUST

Nettle, saltfish and boiled dumplings

250g (½ lb) plain flour

1 cup water

½ teaspoon salt

Nettle and saltfish

1 large tub nettle tops

500g (1lb) saltfish

1 sprig thyme

3 garlic cloves, crushed

1 tablespoon vegetable oil

1 400g tin coconut milk

1 scotch bonnet pepper

1 onion

1 cinnamon stick

2 cloves

Nettle combines well with saltfish. You should be getting a second growth on the nettle you harvested earlier in the year. Or if you dried some in Spring, you can reconstitute with water and use as fresh.   **Serves 4**

1 In a large bowl, mix the flour and salt together. Slowly add the water and work the dough with your hand. The mixture will turn from flour into breadcrumbs and then into a smooth dough. If the dough is too crumbly, add a little more water, if too soggy, add more flour.

2 Form the dough into golf ball shapes, putting a dent in each one, and leave to rest for half an hour. Add the dumplings to a pan of boiling water and boil for 15 minutes.

3 For the nettle and saltfish, boil the saltfish for 5 minutes to remove the salt. Discard the water.

4 Heat the oil and sweat the onion and garlic. Add the scotch bonnet pepper, saltfish, thyme, cinnamon and cloves.

5 Add the chopped nettle leaves and the coconut milk, and stir.

6 Cover the saucepan and simmer for 10 minutes.

7 Serve with the boiled dumplings.

Ash key pickle

2 cups of ash keys, without stalks

1 teaspoon ground cloves

1 teaspoon ground cinnamon

4 bay leaves

8 peppercorns

1 teaspoon allspice

½ teaspoon fresh ginger

1 scotch bonnet pepper, deseeded

1 teaspoon salt

1 tablespoon brown sugar

570ml (1pint) cider vinegar

Make sure that you pick your ash keys when they are very young. You can see the seed if you hold the ash key up to the sunlight. To eat, put the seed side of the key in your mouth and squeeze the seed into your mouth with your teeth. Discard the key which is a bit stringy. They are great with a beer!

1 Wash the ash keys, then place in a pan covered with cold water and bring to the boil. Simmer for 5 minutes. Strain off the water and return to the pan with some fresh water, then bring back to boil and simmer for a further 5 minutes.

2 Drain off the water again, and allow to dry slightly. Pack into warm dry jars, but allow an inch of space from the top of the jar.

3 Put the vinegar and sugar in a saucepan and heat gently to dissolve the sugar.

4 Once dissolved, turn off the heat and add the spices.

5 Pour the spicy vinegar liquid over the ash keys filling the jars right to the brim.

6 Store for 3 months to let the pickle mature. Will keep for years.

AUGUST

Blackberry ice cream

600ml (1 pint) double cream, or dairy free alternative

25g (1oz) caster sugar

100g (4oz) fruit

Blackberry makes the most delicious ice cream! This simple method of making ice cream really works.

1 In a recycled ice cream tub, mash up the washed fruit and the sugar. Add the cream and stir.
2 Put in the freezer for 2 hours. Remove and stir.
3 Repeat this process 2 more times or until the ice cream is solid.

Blackberry Irish moss smoothie

25g (1 oz) Irish moss

50g (2oz) blackberries

1 teaspoon ground cinnamon

1 teaspoon good quality vanilla essence

1 tablespoon ground linseed

60ml (2fl oz) milk

2 tablespoons honey

Irish moss is a seaweed also known as carrageen. It is used as a thickener for desserts as it creates a gel-like liquid. Buy from Caribbean or health food shops, or forage your own on a day trip down to the coast.

1 Soak the Irish moss in 300ml (10fl oz) water for 15 minutes.
2 Add the cinnamon and then boil the Irish moss in this water for 30 minutes.
3 When cooked, drain the Irish moss and discard, reserving the liquid. Add the vanilla essence, washed blackberries, linseed, milk and honey to the moss liquid.
4 Blend well and serve.

AUGUST

Yellow rice and elderberries

100g (4oz) rice

1 small bunch spring onions

3-4 cloves garlic

1 sprig thyme

1 small scotch bonnet pepper, deseeded

½ teaspoon ground allspice

½ teaspoon cloves

1 teaspoon turmeric

1 cup elderberries

Elderberries are a great addition to Caribbean rice. They'll look like a tiny black bean. **Serves 4**

1 Fry the spring onions in a little oil, then add the garlic, thyme, scotch bonnet pepper, allspice, cloves and turmeric.
2 Fry for a couple of minutes. Add the washed rice and water in the quantity of 2 parts water to 1 part rice.
3 Bring the rice mix to the boil, then simmer for 10 minutes or until rice has cooked.
4 Stir in the washed and destalked elderberries just before the rice is cooked. Serve immediately.

To be seen and heard

The walks and feasts operated as a skill share where all participants brought knowledge, curiosity and questions to share with other people. What everyone brought was valued, and seen and heard, as a unique contribution.

"I brought memories of putting dandelion flowers under my brother's pillow to make him wet the bed."

"I brought a life on this estate for twenty years."

"I brought my 8 year old son."

"I brought memories of making tea from mint picked in my grandfather's garden in Scotland."

"I brought knowledge that rosemary is good for your hair as well as for putting in lamb dishes."

"I brought an open mind."

SEPTEMBER

South Asia

Recipes from India, Pakistan, Bangladesh and Sri Lanka

Chestnut and fig *biryani*

Wild herb *pakoras*

Elderberry chutney

Fennel and hogweed seed tea

Apple *jalebi* with wild rose syrup

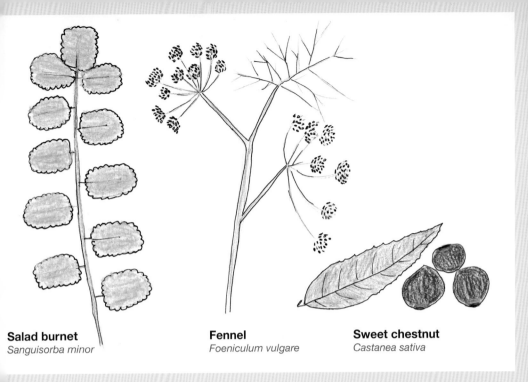

Salad burnet
Sanguisorba minor

Fennel
Foeniculum vulgare

Sweet chestnut
Castanea sativa

Wild food in September

Fennel
What it looks like: It has little umbrellas of mustard yellow flowers and a distinctive aniseed smell. The leaves are feathery.
How it can be useful: Fennel is renowned as a herb for digestion. Fennel seeds are a key ingredient in *mukhwas,* the Indian and Pakistani after-dinner digestive treat.

Salad burnet
What it looks like: It has mid-green soft leaves that are divided into attractive oval-toothed leaflets, reminiscent visually of coriander leaves, although the taste is more like cucumber. It flowers with dark crimson spikes between June and September. You get new growth in September.
How it can be useful: It has traditionally been used to stop bleeding and has an astringent action. It can be a useful addition to winter salads. Use before the flower spikes appear.

Sweet chestnut
What it looks like: It has long, pointed leaves with saw-like teeth. Over the summer, it grows spiky husks in which the nut is housed.
How it can be useful: Chestnuts can be made into puree, pies and porridge, and are a useful wild source of carbohydrate. Please note that horse chestnuts (conkers) cannot be eaten.

Chestnut and fig *biryani*

450g (1lb) basmati rice

1 cup chestnuts

½ cup hazelnuts

5 figs

3 tablespoons oil

2 tablespoons ghee

1 large red onion

1 piece ginger

4 cloves garlic

3 tomatoes

2 bay leaves and chillies

3 cloves

3 cardamom pods

5 black peppercorns

1 stick cinnamon

1 teaspoon coriander seeds and turmeric powder

½ teaspoon garam masala

After some conversations with a friend, Shani, we were inspired to cook *biryani.* She'd seen her mother cook it as a child and shared with me how *biryani* is a dish fit for kings and queens, and is an honour to prepare and eat. We did a one pot version at the Myatt's Fields Park harvest festival. Hazelnuts and figs are normally ready at the end of September in London. Get the nuts before the squirrels do!   Serves 6

1 Soak the rice for at least 15 minutes before cooking.

2 Heat the oil and the ghee in the pan and add the chopped onions. Fry until golden brown. Chop the ginger and garlic and add to the pan. Cook for about 2 minutes.

3 Chop the tomatoes and crush the coriander seeds. Tip in the tomatoes, bay leaves, chillies, cloves, cardamom pods, black peppercorns, cinnamon, turmeric, coriander seeds and garam masala. Cook for a few minutes.

4 Add the nuts and figs.

5 Add the rice and 2 parts water for each part rice. Add salt, cover with a lid and cook for 10 minutes. Check all the water has been absorbed, remove from the heat and leave for a further 5 minutes with the lid still on.

6 Serve with torn salad burnet leaves.

Wild herb *pakoras*

200g (8oz) gram (chick pea) flour

3 tablespoons rice flour (optional)

1 tablespoon coarsely ground coriander

1 teaspoon cumin seeds

1 green chilli

1 teaspoon salt

½ teaspoon baking powder

175ml (6fl oz) water

A large handful of nettle, yarrow and mallow leaves, finely chopped

Vegetable oil to fry

Salad burnet leaves to garnish

Pick whatever herbs are available for these *pakora*. **The addition of the rice flour should make a crispier batter.**
Makes 25 *pakoras*

1 Mix all the dry ingredients together: gram flour, rice flour, coriander powder, baking powder and salt.

2 Add the water slowly to make a smooth batter (batter should be consistency of pancake batter or *dosa* batter).

3 Add the wild herbs and chopped green chilli. Mix well.

4 Heat the oil in a frying pan on medium high heat. (To check if the oil is ready, put one drop of batter in the oil. The batter should float up but not change colour right away).

5 Add 1 tablespoon of the batter per *pakora* to the oil. The *pakoras* will take about 3-4 minutes to cook. Fry until both sides are golden brown, turning occasionally.

6 Remove with a slotted spoon onto absorbent paper.

7 Garnish with salad burnet leaves and serve with chutney.

Elderberry chutney

500g (1lb) elderberries, stripped from stalks

1 small onion, chopped

½ teaspoon salt

½ teaspoon cinnamon

½ teaspoon ground ginger

¼ teaspoon freshly grated nutmeg

½ teaspoon mustard seeds

250ml (½ pint) distilled malt vinegar

1 medium cooking apple, peeled, chopped

50g (2oz) seedless raisins

75g (3oz) soft brown sugar

1 Wash elderberries and put in a thick-bottomed pan with the cinnamon, ginger, mustard seeds, nutmeg, salt and vinegar. Cook very slowly for an hour.

2 Rub the elderberry mixture through a sieve. Return to the pan with the apple, chopped onion, raisins and sugar. Bring slowly to the boil, stirring until sugar has dissolved, then cook in the open pan for 45 minutes, or until the mixture has thickened.

3 Pour into dry, sterilised jars. Put lid on when completely cold. (Plastic coated lids work best so the vinegar doesn't corrode the metal it is in contact with).

4 Leave to mature for 2 months before opening.

Fennel and hogweed seed tea

1 tablespoon fennel
seeds

1 tablespoon hogweed
seeds

Fennel is often an ornamental plant in parks and gardens so if you do pick from them, make sure you ask permission and take only a few seeds from each head to preserve the overall aesthetic look. Hogweed seeds can be picked freely and they bring a spicy cardamom flavour to this tea.

1 Place the seeds in a teapot and fill with boiling water.
2 Leave to steep for 10 minutes and serve.

Apple *jalebi* with wild rose syrup

15-16 apple rings
(apple sliced into thin
wafers, seeds removed)

75g (3oz) plain flour

120ml (4fl oz) lukewarm
water

1 teaspoon dried yeast

2 tablespoons ghee,
melted

1 tablespoon brown
sugar

350ml (12fl oz)
oil for frying

1 tablespoon vanilla
essence

8-10 cashew nuts,
crushed

Rose syrup

50g (2 oz) brown sugar

½ teaspoon saffron
strands

120ml (4fl oz) milk

4 tablespoons lukewarm
water

2 tablespoons rose
petals

1 teaspoon ground
cinnamon

These are fritters soaked in a rose syrup. **Serves 8**

1 To prepare the sugar syrup, put 4 tablespoons water and the milk into a pan and gently bring to the boil.

2 Once boiled, take a few tablespoons of the milk liquid and dissolve the saffron in it. Add the sugar and rose petals to the rest of the milk liquid in the pan.

3 Pour the saffron infused milk back into the pan. Simmer for 10 minutes until the syrup has thickened slightly.

4 For the apple *jalebi,* mix the yeast with the lukewarm water. Stir 1 tablespoon brown sugar into this yeast mixture.

5 When the yeast becomes frothy, add the sifted flour, vanilla essence and the melted ghee. The mixture should be smooth, lump free and a thick consistency. Cover this batter with a cloth and keep aside for 10 minutes.

6 In a deep frying pan, heat the oil until very hot.

7 Dip the apple rings into the batter, drip off excess batter then deep fry the apple rings until golden brown. Place the fried fritters on kitchen roll to absorb excess oil.

8 Lastly, dip the apple rings in the sugar syrup. Soak for a couple of minutes. Repeat the same process with all the apple fritters.

9 Sprinkle with cinnamon powder, cashew nuts and garnish with rose petals. Serve warm or chilled.

Inclusion and connection

"

I love cities, I love the unexpectedness, the variety and the whole mishmash of people in the city. And I also feel sad about the precariousness of the connections that exist between people from different cultural and class backgrounds. There is so much history of being separate and it can be scary stepping out and saying 'I want to connect with you'.

For the South Asian feast, a Bangladeshi family from my son's school came. As well as eating biryani and pakoras, we put bindis on our foreheads, made henna designs on our hands and feet and painted our finger nails blue (for the Libra new moon). Since that day, the mother of the family and I always exchange some words in the school playground, which I enjoy very much.

In the city, you can travel round the world, just by connecting to your neighbour.

"

OCTOBER

South West Europe

Recipes from Portugal, Italy, Spain and France

Wild cabbage and potato soup – *'Caldo Verde'*

Nettle *soufflé*

Chickweed *risotto*

Socca bread with goosegrass seeds and chickweed *pesto*

Pickled sloes

Dandelion bud capers

Rowan fruit cheese

Sloe gin – *'Patxarán!'*

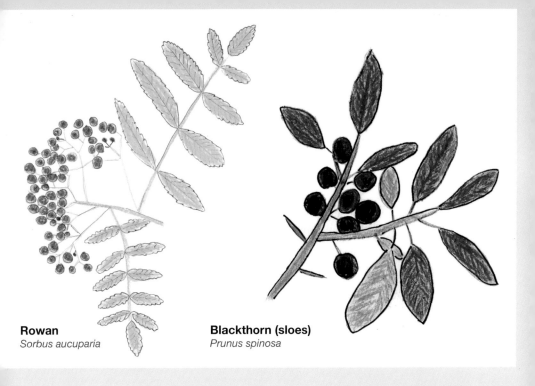

Rowan
Sorbus aucuparia

Blackthorn (sloes)
Prunus spinosa

Wild food in October

Rowan

What it looks like: White 5-petalled flowers appear in May. Leaves comprise many leaflets. Berries hang in bright red or orange bunches from the Summer, throughout the Autumn and into Winter.

How it can be useful: The colourful berries make the tree a great ornamental. Traditionally, rowan is renowned as a magical, protecting tree. Foodwise, it makes an interesting bitter-sweet jelly and wine.

Blackthorn (sloes)

What it looks like: The blackthorn is a dense, many branched shrub with very thorny twigs, so beware when picking.

How it can be useful: Highly astringent (put one in your mouth and see what happens!) Sloes can be made into jellies and as flavouring to spirit drinks. Unripe sloes can also be pickled.

Wild cabbage and potato soup – 'Caldo Verde'

2 onions, chopped

4 cloves garlic, crushed

60ml (2¼ fl oz) olive oil

1 chorizo sausage or vegan chorizo sausage

6 potatoes, diced

1.5l (2 pints) vegetable stock

2 bay leaves

Large bunch of wild cabbage, finely chopped

1 teaspoon smoked paprika

Olive oil

This soup is a popular dish from Portugal, which is perfect for Autumn days. You can substitute the wild cabbage with chickweed or nettle. **Serves 6**

1 Sweat the onions and garlic on a low heat in the olive oil, until they go translucent. Chop the sausage into small chunks and fry, with the onion, for a few minutes. Add the diced potatoes, stock, seasoning and bay leaves, and cook for around 10 minutes until the potatoes are soft.

2 Mash the potatoes in the pan to make the soup thicker.

3 Add the cabbage and simmer for a few minutes.

4 Mix the smoked paprika with some olive oil to make a dressing, and swirl this red mixture into the green and white soup.

5 Serve with some thick, crusty bread.

Nettle *soufflé*

50g (2oz) nettle tops

1 onion, chopped finely

25g (1oz) plain flour

6 eggs

50g (2 oz) parmesan cheese

Olive oil

Salt and pepper to taste

Nettle is a good source of iron, phosphorus, potassium, and B complex vitamins. It also nourishes your respiratory, nervous, urinary, and digestive systems. Makes 4

1 Preheat oven to 200°C (400°F/Gas Mark 6).

2 Blanch the nettles in hot water for a few minutes. Drain and reserve the nutrient rich liquid. Liquidise the nettles.

3 Chop the onion finely and sweat in a little olive oil for 5 minutes, add the flour and cook, stirring constantly for 3 minutes. Add the nettles and 2 tablespoons of the nettle-infused water and cook for a further 3 minutes. Take off the heat.

4 Separate the eggs, and keep the egg whites aside for the next step. Add the egg yolks, together with the grated cheese, to the nettle mixture. Season with salt and pepper, and mix.

5 Grease individual ramekins. Whisk the egg whites until stiff and peaky. Fold them into the nettle mixture. Fill the greased ramekins right to the top and bake for 10 minutes.

6 Serve immediately otherwise they'll deflate. Soufflé goes very well with a salad.

Chickweed *risotto*

170g (6oz) chickweed

1l (2 pints) vegetable stock

2 tablespoons olive oil

1 large onion, finely chopped

2 cloves garlic, finely chopped

400g (14oz) risotto rice

Sea salt and freshly ground black pepper

50g (2oz) butter

115g (4oz) freshly grated parmesan cheese

1 teaspoon fresh thyme leaves

1 lemon (you need the zest)

Always use a heavy-bottomed pan, especially if you're cooking outside on a stove that is difficult to regulate. I burnt this dish horribly once in Ruskin Park, using a thin-bottomed pan. I was heartened by the wonderful people I was cooking for who didn't seem to mind and said 'it doesn't matter'. Some of them even ate it! **Serves 6**

1 In a heavy-bottomed pan, heat the olive oil, add the onions and garlic and fry very slowly for 10 minutes.

2 Add the rice and turn up the heat slightly. Keep stirring the rice. After a minute, the rice will look slightly translucent.

3 Add a ladle of the hot stock to the rice mixture. Turn down the heat to a simmer. Add the thyme and lemon zest. Keep adding ladlefuls of stock, stirring and allowing each ladleful to be absorbed before adding the next. This will take around 25-30 minutes until the rice is soft but with a slight bite. When the rice is almost done, add the chopped chickweed. If you run out of stock before the rice is cooked, add some boiling water.

4 Remove from the heat and add the butter and parmesan. Stir well. Place a lid on the pan and allow to sit for 2 minutes so the risotto can become creamy.

5 Serve and garnish with chickweed.

Socca bread with goosegrass seeds and chickweed *pesto*

400g (14 oz) gram (chickpea) flour

800ml (27fl oz) water

1 teaspoon salt

4 tablespoons olive oil

Freshly ground black pepper

1 tablespoon goosegrass seeds

Pesto

50g (2oz) pine nuts

200g (8oz) fresh chickweed leaves

100g (4oz) parmesan cheese, grated

300ml (10fl oz) olive oil

1 teaspoon sea salt

2 cloves garlic, crushed

Socca bread, also called *farinata* in Italy, is a kind of flat bread made from chickpea flour. It's a typical street food of the Ligurian coast, from Nice to Pisa, and is baked in large outdoor ovens in market places. Here, I've given instructions for frying the bread like a pancake.   **Makes 10 pancakes**

1 To make the batter, sift the gram flour into a bowl and whisk in the water, salt and olive oil until smooth.
2 Toast the goosegrass seeds until dark brown. Crush them finely and add half to the batter mixture.
3 Heat some oil in a frying pan on a medium heat. When the oil starts to smoke, pour back the excess oil into a ceramic bowl. Pour enough batter into the pan to thinly cover the bottom. Cook for 3-4 minutes or until the batter has hardened on one side. Flip over with a fish slice. Cook for another 3-4 minutes, then remove.
4 Return the saved oil to the pan. Heat again until just starting to smoke, then remove the excess and add more batter to make the next pancake.
5 Slice the pancakes into pieces. Serve with plenty of black pepper, a sprinkle of goosegrass seeds and chickweed *pesto*.

Pesto
1 Grind nuts until fine and chop herbs very finely.
2 Mix nuts and herbs together with the oil, cheese, and salt and pepper. This *pesto* will keep for up to a week in the fridge.

Pickled sloes and dandelion bud capers

500g (1lb) sloes

2 shallots

2-3 garlic cloves

1 teaspoon spices (peppercorns, coriander seeds, dill seeds and a bay leaf)

750ml (1¼ pints) pickling or white wine vinegar

Dandelion bud capers

A cup of dandelion buds

½ teaspoon peppercorns

½ teaspoon juniper berries

Sea salt

A revolutionary replacement for the olive! Sloes are best stored in jars. The easiest way to sterilise glass is in the oven set to 130°C (275°F/Gas Mark 1) for 20 minutes.

1 Wash the sloes. Pack them, along with the chopped shallots, garlic and spices, into fresh, clean, sterilised jars.

2 Fill the jars with vinegar to cover the sloes.

3 Shake once a week and try them after a month. They will keep for at least a year.

4 Serve as an appetiser. Don't eat the stones inside the sloe.

Dandelion bud capers

1 Wash and rinse a cupful of buds and pack them in a glass jar with some juniper berries and peppercorns.

2 Sprinkle salt generously over the contents and fill with water. Leave for a week, shaking regularly. Serve on top of pizza.

Rowan fruit cheese

1kg (2¼ lb) rowan berries

Juice of a lemon

450g (1lb) jam sugar (high in pectin)

1 sprig of thyme

It's called a 'cheese' but is more like a jelly, and it's good served with cheese. Rowan is strong and bitter tasting (you either love it or hate it). Alternatively, use crab apples or if you want to use quinces, go to a Portuguese shop.

1 Wash the rowan berries and place in a preserving pan with 600ml (1 pint) water. Add the lemon juice, bring to the boil and simmer for around 20 minutes or until the fruit is all mushy.

2 Sieve the juice from the saucepan into a bowl. Use a wooden spoon to get as much juice out as you can.

3 Measure the juice. For each 450ml (15fl oz), add 450g (1lb) sugar. For example, if you have 350ml (12.5fl oz) juice, add 350g (12oz) sugar.

4 Put the juice and sugar mixture back in the pan. Dissolve the sugar gently, then bring to the boil and simmer for 40 minutes. Be careful it doesn't burn.

5 Do the same test as for jam by placing a spoonful of mixture on a chilled plate and drawing your finger through it. It needs to create a clearer trail than for jam and will be a thicker consistency.

6 Spread the mixture in flat trays which you have lined with greaseproof paper. Leave it to cool, then cut into desired sizes.

7 Serve with icing sugar finely sprinkled on top and with thyme.

Sloe gin – 'Patxarán!'

70cl (25fl oz) bottle
of gin (cheap is fine)

125g (5oz) sugar

220g (8oz) sloes

On one of the walks, while talking with Marga Burgui-Artajo, we discovered a connection between sloe gin and *patxarán* of the Basque country. *Patxarán* is made by macerating sloes in anisette, a liqueur made from distilling aniseed. Marga got some sent over for our end-of-year celebration and we also had a London version, made with gin of course.

1 Decant the bottle of gin into a jug.
2 To get the sloes' juices flowing, prick the washed sloes with a needle and pop them into the empty gin bottle. Alternatively, you could freeze the sloes for a night.
3 Add the sugar through a funnel (or a sheet of paper curled into a cone shape).
4 Return the gin to the bottle of sloes. You'll now have more gin than you have room for in this bottle so fill another empty bottle with extra sloes, sugar and the remaining gin.
5 From time to time, give the bottle a shake. Leave for at least three months before serving.

Contribution

" Every one of us has something to offer our community through sharing our life experience, our skills or our unique approach. Very often this may be something that we don't anticipate or even value. People have enriched the walks and feasts by playing with the children, helping with washing up, having a propensity to joke around and be expansive, or conversely contributing quietness or the ability to listen.

It's also a contribution to be the only man in a group of women, or to be the only person of your colour in the group.

Very often, just showing up is a huge contribution. "

NOVEMBER

South East Europe

Recipes from Greece, Turkey and the Balkans

Nettle soup

Wild herb *falafel* with daisy
and sorrel leaf *tzatziki*

Hot elderberry drink

Dandelion *spanakopita* pie

Rosehip rice pudding – '*Zerde*'

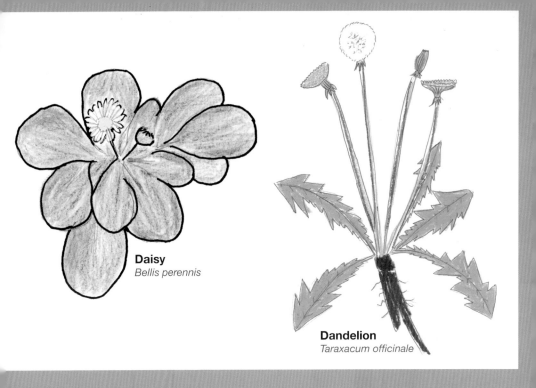

Daisy
Bellis perennis

Dandelion
Taraxacum officinale

Wild food in November

Daisy
What it looks like: Daisies are low growing with leaves that form a basal rosette. They have many-petalled white flowers, some with a pink tinge to their edges, which flowers throughout the year.
How it can be useful: The leaves, especially, are high in vitamin C and can grow large enough to make harvesting worthwhile. The flowers can be eaten but aren't very tasty, but you can use the petals, individually strewn, as garnish.

Dandelion
What it looks like: There are many different varieties. Sharply-lobed leaves form a basal rosette. Sunshine-yellow flowers, made up of 200 florets, close at night. Buds are to be found in the centre of the rosette.
How it can be useful: You can eat the leaves, the flowers, the buds and the root. Eating a few dandelion greens will assist the digestive process. The greens are very high in vitamins A and C, potassium, calcium, iron, phosphorous, and B complex vitamins. Dandelion root supports the liver. The traditional Greek dish *Horta,* is made from briefly boiled dandelion and nettle leaves, dressed with olive oil, lemon and salt and pepper.

Nettle soup

450g (1lb) nettle tops

1l (1.5 pints) water

2 potatoes, diced

1 onion, chopped

60ml (2fl oz) single cream or non-dairy cream

2 tablespoons oil

1 teaspoon sea salt

The addition of potatoes to this nettle soup makes it thicker and creamier. If you want to make it without potatoes, it is darker and more intense. Add less water so it's not too thin. It's still possible to get fresh nettles in November but make sure the new growth hasn't yet flowered.   **Serves 4**

1 Heat 2 tablespoons oil and gently fry the chopped onion. Add the diced potatoes, the nettles, salt and the water. Bring to the boil and simmer for 10 minutes or until the potatoes are soft.
2 Liquidise and add the cream to serve.

Wild herb *falafel* with daisy and sorrel leaf *tzatziki*

75g (3oz) red lentils

400g (14oz) tin chick peas

75g (3oz) bulgur wheat

2 tablespoons olive oil

1 onion, finely chopped

1 teaspoon cumin

1 tablespoon tomato paste

1 tablespoon paprika

juice of 1 lemon

50g (2oz) wild herbs (dandelion, yarrow, nettle)

50g (2oz) daisy leaves

Tzatziki

350g (12oz) Greek yoghurt

25g (1oz) daisy and sorrel leaves

¼ stick of cucumber

2 tablespoons lemon juice

2 cloves of garlic, crushed

1 teaspoon olive oil

½ teaspoon paprika

Tzatziki is called *cacik* in Turkey and *tarator* in the Balkans.
Makes 30 *falafel*

1 To make the *tzatziki*, peel the cucumber and grate. Put the gratings in a tea towel and squeeze out the excess liquid.

2 Chop the daisy and sorrel leaves, reserving some for a garnish.

3 Combine the yoghurt, cucumber, lemon juice, chopped leaves and the garlic. Add a dash of olive oil and place in the fridge until you need it.

4 To make the *falafel*, cook the lentils in 240ml (8fl oz) water with 1 teaspoon salt for 15 minutes. Similarly, cook the bulgar wheat in a separate pan, in the same amount of water and salt.

5 While lentils and wheat are cooking, heat the oil in a pan and gently fry the onion for 5 minutes.

6 Add the cumin, paprika, lemon juice and tomato paste and cook for a further 5 minutes. Add the tomato and onion mixture to the lentils and bulgar wheat.

7 Wash the wild herbs well, chop and add to the mixture. Add chick peas. Liquidise everything into a smooth paste.

8 Take about 2 tablespoons of the mixture and form into round balls. If the mixture is too sticky to form a ball, sieve gram (chick-pea) flour in slowly until the mixture binds.

9 Shallow fry the *falafel*. Sprinkle the *tzatziki* with paprika and whole daisy leaves. Serve both with pitta bread.

Hot elderberry drink

500g (1lb) elderberries

2 tablespoons honey

Juice and zest of
1 lemon

1 small piece of
cinnamon stick

1 small piece ginger,
chopped

½ teaspoon allspice
berries

A grating of nutmeg

Mulled wine dates back to Ancient Greece where wine, red or white, was spiced, sweetened with honey and served hot as a tonic. This is a great immune system boosting drink which you can drink all throughout the winter. I find freezing elderberries in small batches the best way of preserving them.

1 Put the elderberries in a pan with 4-5 tablespoons water, the cinnamon, the ginger, the allspice and a grating of nutmeg.
2 Bring to boil then simmer over a low heat for 15 minutes.
3 Sieve the berries and put the juice in a clean pan with the honey, lemon juice and zest. Simmer for 5 minutes. Retrieve the cinnamon stick and keep it in the drink for decoration. Serve hot.

Dandelion *spanakopita*

250g (9oz) plain flour

4 tablespoons olive oil

½ teaspoon sea salt

1 teaspoon vinegar

120ml (4fl oz) warm water

Filling

450g (1lb) dandelion and nettle leaves

1 onion, finely chopped

2 tablespoons olive oil

2 cloves garlic, chopped

2 eggs

170g (6oz) feta cheese

½ teaspoon ground black pepper

½ teaspoon sea salt

60ml (2fl oz) water

This dish is often made with filo pasty and can be shaped into triangles. However, it's also possible on some Greek islands to find this recipe using shortcrust pastry.   **Serves 6**

1 To prepare the pastry, combine flour, salt, olive oil and vinegar in a large mixing bowl.

2 Slowly add the water to the flour mixture to make a soft dough. You may not need all the water. Knead for 2 minutes. If it is too dry, add a little more water. Shape into a ball and cover with plastic wrap. Put in the fridge.

3 Preheat oven to 180°C (350°F/Gas Mark 4).

4 To prepare the filling, heat the oil on medium heat, add the chopped garlic and fry for a minute. Add onions, salt and pepper and fry for 3-4 minutes until onions are translucent.

5 Add the greens and water. Cook for 5 minutes and allow to cool.

6 Grease the pie dish. Roll out the dough so it's bigger than the pie dish. Pick up the sheet of dough with the rolling pin and press into the shape of the pan. Slice the pastry off with a knife to get it the right size.

7 Crack eggs and crumble feta cheese into the greens mixture. Place this mixture on top of the dough and spread evenly.

8 Roll out the remaining pastry and place it over the pie dish and filling. Slice the pastry off and press the edges together to seal.

9 Bake for 25-30 minutes until golden brown. Leave to cool slightly after taking out the oven. Slice and serve.

NOVEMBER

Rosehip rice pudding – 'Zerde'

110g (4oz) pudding rice

1l (1.75 pints) water

2 tablespoons cornflour

85g (3oz) sugar

1 tablespoon rose water

30ml (2fl oz) rosehip syrup (see December)

2 cardamom pods

A few sprigs of marjoram

1 Soak saffron in 2 tablespoons of the water and wait for 15 minutes until the water goes yellow.

2 Wash rice very well and bring to the boil in 850ml (29fl oz) water. Crush the cardamom pods and add seeds to the pan. Simmer for around 20 minutes.

3 Pour the yellow water into the rice. Mix the cornflour with what's left of the litre of water, which should be around 140ml (5fl oz). Add sugar and rose water to the cornflour mix and add this to the pan of rice and simmer for another 5 minutes.

4 Divide the rice pudding into small cups and serve it hot or cold. Pour over 1 tablespoon of rosehip syrup into each cup and garnish with marjoram leaves.

Appreciation

"*The walks and feasts operated as a skill share where all participants brought knowledge, curiosity and questions to share with other people. From this wealth of experience, everyone took away something they valued or appreciated; whether that was some knowledge or the experience of connection or inspiration.*

"Today I took away mallow which I'm going to boil up as a vegetable."

"Today I took away some rosemary to wash my hair with."

"Today I took away the taste of wild rocket, both leaf and flower. Strong and sweet!"

"Today I took away a conversation with my neighbours."

"Today I took away a good community spirit."

"Today I took away a hope to come again.""

Central and South America

Recipes from Brazil, Colombia, Venezuela and Peru

Wild herb cheese bread – *'Pão de Queijo'*

Plantain seed and wild cabbage winter stew

Dock leaf polenta wrap – *'Hallaca'*

Chilli chocolate cake with rosehip syrup

High vitamin C rosehip drink

Rosehip syrup

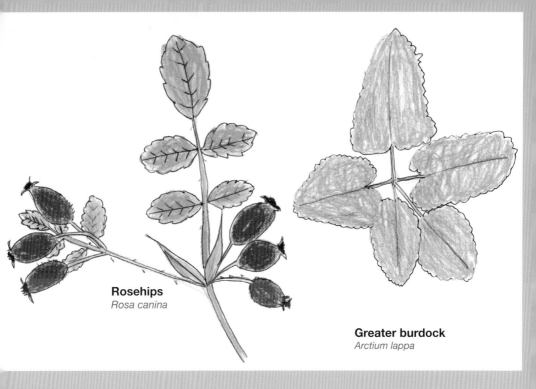

Rosehips
Rosa canina

Greater burdock
Arctium lappa

Wild food in December

Rosehips
What it looks like: The rose bush has long, arching stems that are covered with hooked thorns. The smooth, oval, red rosehips with tufty bits at their tops appear from September and stay on the bush throughout the Winter. You can still pick them after they've become squishy.
How it can be useful: Very high in vitamin C. Rosehips can be made into jellies and cordials.

Greater burdock
What it looks like: Large, arching grey-green leaves, cottony on underside, form in a rosette in the first year while the tap root burrows into the ground. It's a biannual plant that grows tall in its second year when it shoots out the burrs that stick to clothes. Burdock burrs are the inspiration for Velcro.
How it can be useful: Dig up the roots at the end of the first year or at the beginning of the second while all the nutrients are still concentrated in the roots. The root is esteemed in both Chinese and Western herbal medicine as a detoxifying herb. You can steam and eat the young tender leaves.

Wild herb cheese bread – *'Pão de Queijo'*

500g (18oz) manioc starch flour

350ml (12fl oz) milk

30ml (2fl oz) oil

2 eggs

200g (8oz) grated cheese

1 teaspoon salt

Finely chopped wild herbs (yarrow, salad burnet, chickweed)

You can get manioc starch flour in Portuguese or Brazilian shops. It's the very finely milled flour from the cassava root. Tapioca starch flour works just as well and you can get this in a Chinese supermarket. **Makes 30 balls**

1 Preheat oven to 200°C (390°F/Gas Mark 4).

2 Combine the milk and oil in a pan and scald (scald means heat to just below boiling point). Pour onto the flour in a bowl and let cool slightly.

3 Add the other ingredients and knead to form a dough. It should be smooth and silky to touch. If it's too sticky, add more flour, if it's too dry, add milk in tiny amounts to get the consistency right.

4 Roll the dough into small balls 3cm in diameter. Smooth the balls by rolling around in the palm of your hand for a few seconds.

5 Put the balls on a greased baking tray and bake for around 12-15 minutes or until golden.

6 Serve with cream cheese or a spicy sauce.

Plantain seed and wild cabbage winter stew

250g (8oz) carioca
beans, soaked overnight
in plenty of water

1 onion, finely chopped

5 cloves garlic, finely
chopped

1 handful wild herbs,
finely chopped (yarrow,
nettle, salad burnet)

1 cup of ribwort or
greater plantain seeds,
ground

4 bay leaves

Carioca beans are a slightly speckled light caramel brown colour, but you could experiment with any bean. This dish is based on a recipe from Minas Gerais in Brazil, although many dishes throughout the continent share aspects of this hearty dish. **Serves 6**

1 To cook the beans, bring to the boil, then simmer for about an hour until soft. Keep them in their liquid.
2 In a frying pan, fry the onion and garlic until soft.
3 Add the beans in their cooking liquid, salt and bay leaves, to the frying pan and simmer for 15 minutes.
4 Add the wild herbs and the ground plantain seeds to the mixture and cook for another 5 minutes.
5 Serve with rice and a few cheese breads on the side.

Dock leaf polenta wrap – 'Hallaca'

Massa (dough)

1 teaspoon elderberries

500g (1lb) polenta flour

1 teaspoon salt

1 teaspoon cayenne pepper

Olive oil

300ml (10oz) warm water

This Christmas dish from Central America brings together European traditions with the dried fruits and olives, Native American traditions in the cornmeal and African traditions with the banana leaves. We substitute banana leaves with greater burdock leaves. Makes 10 *hallacas*

When I interviewed Maria Alexandra from Venezuela, about the dish, she said "When I think of hallaca, I think of the sound of dominoes, I think of my father and grandfather drunk because they drink from early, and of my mother always complaining about them. I always cried when I had to peel the onions. 'Peeling onions is good for your nails. When you ground the corn, your breasts are gonna grow, and if you mix the eggs and they go high, you gonna be good in bed' my grandmother said."

In this wild food vegetarian version, you have the chance to bring all the wonderful things you've pickled and preserved into one extravagant dish.

1 To make the sauce, heat two tablespoons of olive oil in a medium pan and add the cumin seeds. Add the chopped onion, 2 spring onions and 2 garlic cloves, and fry for 5 minutes.
2 Chop the tomatoes and red pepper, and add to the onions. Add soy sauce and chopped chilli. Add the red wine and let the sauce simmer for another 5 minutes.

Fillings and sauce

25g (1oz) walnuts

25g (1oz) hazelnuts

25g (1oz) chestnuts

25g (1oz) beech nuts

50g (2oz) rowan cheese
(see October)

2 tablespoons pickled
sloes (see October)

2 tablespoons
dandelion bud capers
(see October)

2 small onions, chopped

4-5 cloves garlic

6 brussels sprouts

4 large tomatoes

1 red pepper

4 spring onions, chopped

1 teaspoon each of
black peppercorns,
coriander seeds,
cumin seeds

1 teaspoon elderberries

1 chilli

Soy sauce

3 tablespoons red wine
(optional)

500g (1lb) polenta flour

1 tablespoon cornflour

Packaging

10 large dock leaves
(20–30cm long)

String

Aluminium foil

3 Remove 2 tablespoons of the sauce into a cup and add 1 table-spoon cornflour to this. Stir until smooth and return to the pan. Simmer for another 3-4 minutes to thicken. This is your **sauce.**

4 **To prepare the fillings,** scald the beech nuts by placing them in near boiling water for 5 minutes, then remove outer shell. Pierce the chestnuts and boil for 15 minutes. Toast all the nuts and put in a bowl.

5 Put the pickled olives, dandelion capers and rowan cheese (cubed into tiny pieces) in separate bowls.

6 Chop the sprouts and steam for 5 minutes. Put aside in a bowl.

7 **To prepare the polenta,** warm 2 tablespoons olive oil with the elderberries in a pan for 10 minutes. The oil should turn red.

8 While this is warming, heat 2 tablespoons oil in a separate pan, add black pepper and coriander seeds. Chop 1 onion, 2 spring onions and 2 garlic cloves, and add to the pan. Add 1l (1.75 pints) of boiling water. Season well. Simmer this broth for 15 minutes.

9 Strain the broth (discarding waste) into a large bowl and add the red oil (having removed the elderberries).

10 Add the polenta slowly to this broth, stirring very well. A dough will form with a smooth consistency.

11 Make a small dough test. Wrap 1 teaspoon dough in a small segment of dock leaf. Wrap this parcel in aluminium foil and boil for 10 minutes. If the cooked dough maintains the shape of the dock leaf package, the dough is perfect. If it crumbles into the water, add more polenta flour.

12 **To wrap and boil the** *hallacas.* Wash the dock leaves. Blanch them for 1 minute in boiling water to soften them.

13 Cut a 30cm piece of aluminium foil. Place a dock leaf on the foil and rub oil on the silvery inside of the leaf facing you. Put half a ladle of polenta in the centre of the leaf. Spread with a spoon to create a 10cm x 5cm rectangle.

14 Put 1 tablespoon of sauce on top of the polenta and a tea-spoon of each filling on top of this.

15 Tuck in the sides of the dock leaves and wrap up the dock leaf and polenta layers, ensuring the sauce and fillings are enclosed within the polenta. Wrap foil around the whole packet. Tie with kitchen string. Boil the *hallacas* in water for 20-30 minutes.

16 Serve the *hallacas* and get the dominoes out.

Chilli chocolate cake with rosehip syrup

230ml (8fl oz) soya milk

1 teaspoon apple cider vinegar

1 teaspoon vanilla extract

90ml (3fl oz) sunflower oil (or similar)

75g (3oz) caster sugar

225g (8oz) self raising flour

75g (3oz) cocoa powder

1 teaspoon baking powder

½ teaspoon chilli powder

The Aztecs considered chocolate so valuable, they used it as currency. This is a dairy-free cake. It generally needs to be eaten on the day you cook it, and it's great served straight out of the oven.

1 Preheat oven to 180°C (350°F/Gas Mark 4) and grease the tin.
2 Whisk the vinegar into the milk to make it curdle. After a few minutes, add vanilla extract, oil and sugar. Beat until foamy.
3 In a separate bowl, sift the flour, cocoa powder, baking powder and chilli powder. Mix all the ingredients together.
4 Mix the dry and wet ingredients together. Put the mixture into the tin. For best results, get your cake in the oven straight away.
5 To make the rosehip syrup, follow the instructions on page 118.
6 Serve the cake with hot syrup generously poured over.

High vitamin C rosehip drink

1 kg (2lbs) rosehips

2 sprigs of lavender

2 x 2l water

A northern version of the tropical acerola juice; acerola berries have a massive 2,330mg vitamin C per 100g serving. Rosehips have 425mg per 100g which is still higher than oranges and blackcurrants. Rosehip syrup was produced on a large scale during wartime Britain. The rosehips have their own sweetness so I tend not to add sugar. This drink will keep for about a week in the fridge.   Makes 1.5 litres

1 Boil the rosehips and one sprig of lavender in the water for around 20 minutes.
2 Drain the rosehips, and save the water in a container.
3 Repeat the process with the same rosehips and the second batch of water and the second sprig of lavender.
4 Combine the two batches of rosehip water and mix well.
5 Serve hot or cold.

DECEMBER

Rosehip syrup

1 kg (2lbs) rosehips

2 sprigs of lavender

2 x 2l water

450g (1lb) sugar

You can also make a syrup out of sloes in the same way. Star anise, cloves, cinnamon bark and rosemary all work well as flavourings for the highly astringent sloe.   **Makes 1 litre**

1 Boil the rosehips and one sprig of lavender in the water for around 20 minutes.

2 Drain the rosehips, and save the water.

3 Repeat the process with the same rosehips and the second batch of water and the second sprig of lavender.

4 Add 450g (1lb) sugar to the combined rosehip waters and put on a low heat to dissolve.

5 Increase the heat and simmer for 15 minutes to thicken.

6 Serve over Chilli chocolate cake.

Trust

> *While contemplating writing this book, I was overwhelmed by a fear that 'No one's going to be interested in this.' Feedback from potential publishers along the lines of 'What is this? ... a recipe book or a book about community?' compounded my fears.*
>
> *What I needed was to strengthen my sense of trust that connection to each other and to nature matters. I remembered the faces of the people who came on the walks month after month, I remembered the feeling of relaxation, lost in time, while picking blackberries, and I remembered the longing for connection with my neighbours, deep inside me, which drove this project.*

Thank you
to those who contributed to the publishing fund

Ozichi Brewster, Judy Wong, Colin and Chris Triplow, White Rose, Angela Brew, Irina Borowski, Beamish & McGlue of West Norwood, Carol Wragg, Marina Quay, Rachel Anderson, Nora Ganescu, Marga Burgui-Artajo, Cynthia Roomes, Martha Brown, John and Carol Buckmaster, Chris and Nicky Buckmaster, Thelma Sharma, Nancy Oken, Kim Bullock, Rose Agnew, Andy Pattenden, Malcolm Andeson, John Cannell, Elaine Andresier, Stefanie Lotter, Martin Laqué, Francois Beausoleil, Tamar Yoseloff, Abbott Chrisman, Ann Bodkin, Albert Pellicer, Brixton Cornercopia, Aleksandra Magdziarek, Helen Mitcham, Kate Duncan, Catherine Touhy, Pat Kahn, Karine Audeguy, Dorothea Bohlius, Rhonda Booth, Rita Macieg, Billie Jeyes, James Friel, Liz Reynolds, Marion Brown, Tori and Phil Sherwin, Aga Mielewicz, Margaret Swiatly, Dorota Jasina, Mags Smith, Rashda and Hamid, Ibuki Iwata, Sam Furlonger, Sophie Reynolds, Russell Page, Eric Hoekstra, Kay Pitcher, Jayne Middleton, Terra Incognita, Karl Smerecnik, Kate Gallon and Elen Jones, Paul and Heather, Sue Holper, Sam Jarvis and Andres Sampedro, Joyce from Wimbledon, Cassie Pearse, Virginia Nimarkoh, Ali Mullen, Regina Bastos, Rosella Salari, Sue Sheehan, Julie Higgins, Mary Wright, Mindy Cox, Ada and Rok Praprotnik, Fergus Drennan, Anne Marie and Tubbs, Emma Allotey, Elma Glasgow, Jason Gibilaro, Jasper Sharp, Zana, Anthea Masey, Sara Haglund, Fan Sissoko, Roy Vickery, Viveka Gardens, Paul de Zylva, Filippo Laurenti, Kalpana Lal, Sue Bell, Miguel Santos, Fiona Graham, David Robert and Fiona Houghton, Nick Neale, Patricia Curtiss, Louisa Jane Reece, Emily Smith, David Wickstead, Richard Gray, Ruth Standring, Fiona Takahashi, Tate Modern, Roots and Shoots, Iratxe Gardoki, Vivienne Thompson, Turan Holland, Edinburgh Foody, Julia Lally, Mandy Mazliah, Manya Lindsay, Arnaud Tiberghien, Alice Tyler, Chris Elllins, Maria Galanti and those who preferred not to be mentioned.

What everyone brought was valued, and seen and heard, as a unique contribution.

Special thanks
This project would not have begun were it not for Rachel Anderson, at Artangel Interaction, who commissioned Invisible Food in the first instance, and the work of Judy Wong CBE, Director of Black Environment Network. The project would not have continued in the way it did without the support of Jorge Goia, Ramya Lindsay, Segen Ghebrekidan, Victoria Sherwin at Myatt's Fields Park and all those who regularly turned up for walks. Special mention to Martha Brown for beyond-the-call-of-duty proofreading, and Gary Chesterman at Media CPM for warm, expert support when preparing the book for print. Finally, the book would not have been written without Kate Gallon, Mags Smith, Jayne Middleton, Karl Smerecnik, Shani Choudhari, and Rachel Anderson, and that special night in October 2012 when we gathered to discuss the support I needed to get the book done.

Resources

Wild food and Environment

Books
(the four I found most useful)

Food for free by Richard Mabey
Wild food by Roger Phillips
The forager handbook by Miles Irving
Wild fermentation by Sandor Ellix Katz

Learning
Fergus Drennan is a wild food experimentalist and educator, and runs full day foraging courses for the general public (and I did a few with him). He is currently spending a year eating a 100% wild food diet.
www.fergustheforager.co.uk

Foraging courses around Britain with Robin Harford.
www.eatweeds.co.uk

The Wildlife Trusts are nature conservation charities that run day courses in plant identification.
www.wildlifetrusts.org

The Black Environment Network (BEN) works to enable full ethnic participation in the built and natural environment. It represents ethnic issues through influencing policy and fuelling debate, and raises awareness about the significance of the contribution of ethnic communities.
www.ben-network.org.uk

Community
Nonviolent Communication (NVC) is based on the principles of nonviolence. NVC begins by assuming that we are all compassionate by nature and that violent strategies, whether verbal or physical, are learned behaviors taught and supported by the prevailing culture. NVC also assumes that we all share the same, basic human needs.
www.cnvc.org
www.nvc-uk.com

A restorative circle is a community process for supporting people in conflict around the world.
www.restorativecircles.org

Index